D1557306

SURVEY OF THE SCRIPTURES
BASIC BIBLE COMMENTARY

Acts

Power for Witnessing

Dr. Alfred Martin

MERIDIAN
PUBLICATIONS

*C*ontents

Preface

To begin to understand the specifics of in-depth Bible study, we need a picture of how the entire Bible fits together.

The *Survey of the Scriptures* series is a tour through the Bible that points out how one section relates to another, each subject to the whole. By knowing how each part relates to the others, we can better appreciate and apply its lessons for us. Then the series concentrates on individual books of the Bible.

Meridian titles in addition to *Acts—Power for Witnessing* in the *Survey of the Scriptures* currently include:

The New Testament—Matthew through Revelation

Matthew—Gospel of the King

John—Life through Believing

Romans—Amazing Grace

Revelation—God's Final Word to Man

Additional titles in the *Survey of the Scriptures* series are forthcoming.

For many years Dr. Alfred Martin taught these *Survey of the Scriptures* as "Bible 101" at Moody Bible Institute and then later at Dallas Bible Institute and at Southern Bible Institute. For over thirty years the summary of his work has been published as a Bible correspondence course for the External Studies Division of Moody Bible Institute.

Now for the first time, this incisive and insightful study of Acts is available for personal or group Bible study, providing a more in-depth look at the book than the general surveys in the *Survey of the Scriptures* series.

More than thirty years ago I graduated from Moody Bible Institute with a foundation in God's Word built on *Survey of the Scriptures*. As Dr. Martin then opened up for me a new understanding and appreciation of the Bible, I now am proud to be able to publish his survey materials so that you too can better appreciate how each portion of God's Word fits into the whole.

—The Publisher

*I*ntroduction

To see the Bible as a whole is not only vital to a proper understanding of the Bible; it is also a thrilling experience!

Survey of the Scriptures, first written as a Bible study course by Dr. Alfred Martin, Vice President and Dean of Education Emeritus of Moody Bible Institute, Chicago, is based in part on a former course by Dr. James M. Gray, past president of Moody Bible Institute. Dr. Martin quotes Dr. Gray throughout the *Survey*. Maps and charts were prepared by John Phillips, author of several of the *Exploring the Scriptures* titles. John Phillips was director of both Moody and Emmaus correspondence schools.

In addition to the general *Survey* books, this book and others provide study material on individual books of the Bible for a closer look at specific areas of Scripture.

Acts was written by Luke as a continuation of his gospel and records the final acts of Jesus and the beginnings of the fulfillment of the Great Commission.

This commentary, rather than being a complete study of the Acts, is an introduction to help you get started on a lifetime of Bible study and Christian growth.

Because these materials were initially used both as classroom and correspondence school texts, Dr. Martin's style is one of a teacher—guiding, challenging, directing, stimulating, and raising questions as well as providing answers.

Various ways of studying the Bible are suggested for further study. This book can be used as a quarterly reading guide or for individual or group Bible study.

The content of this edition is taken from an adult credit course from Moody Bible Institute, External Studies Division. For information on how you might take this and other courses for credit, write for a free catalog to:

Moody External Studies
Moody Bible Institute
820 N. La Salle
Chicago, IL 60610

1

What the Lord Jesus Continued to Do

Acts 1–2

The book which is called the Acts of the Apostles was written by Luke as a continuation of his gospel. In the introduction Luke tells us how in the "former account" he made known "all that Jesus began both to do and teach" (Acts 1:1 NKJV). From this wording it is logical to assume that Acts tells of the continuing ministry of the risen Lord Jesus Christ, working by his Holy Spirit through the apostles and other believers. We may look at the New Testament this way:

What Jesus began both to do and teach—the Gospels

What Jesus continued to do—the Acts

What Jesus continued to teach—the Epistles and the Revelation

We may expect then that this book will contain the record of some of those deeds which the Lord Jesus promised his disciples they would perform when he said:

"Most assuredly, I say to you, he who believes in Me, the works that I do he will do also; and greater works than these he will do, because I go to My Father" (John 14:12 NKJV).

A BOOK OF WITNESSING

Acts is preeminently a book of witnessing, following the plan laid down by the Lord Jesus Christ in his last interview with the disciples before his ascension to heaven. He said:

"But you shall receive power when the Holy Spirit has come upon you; and you shall be witnesses to Me in Jerusalem, and in all Judea and Samaria, and to the end of the earth" (Acts 1:8 NKJV).

The first main division of the book tells of the witness in Jerusalem, Judea, and Samaria (chapters 1–12); the second division tells of the witness to the ends of the earth (chapters 13–28).

A BOOK OF ACTIVE CHRISTIANS

The title of the book is not a part of the inspired text but was given at a very early date. Actually we are told nothing in the book about the acts of most of the apostles. The majority are not mentioned after the listing of their names among those in the upper room before Pentecost (Acts 1:13).

The story in Acts revolves mainly around Peter and Paul. The first part describes the ministry of Peter and others, principally to the Jews, from the center in Jerusalem (chapters 1–12). The second part portrays the ministry of Paul and others, principally to the Gentiles, from the new center of missionary activity in Antioch (chapters 13–28).

Acts is a book of the stirring deeds of men and women filled with the Holy Spirit. While Peter and Paul dominate the record, attention is given to Stephen, the first martyr; Philip, the deacon and the evangelist of Samaria; Barnabas, the befriender of Paul; Silas, the missionary companion; Aquila and Priscilla, coworkers with Paul and instructors of Apollos; and others. Luke himself is there in the "we" sections (Acts 16:10–17; 20:6–21; 18; 27:1–28:16).

A BOOK OF SPEECHES

Acts is a book of sermons and addresses, delivered on all sorts of occasions under widely varying circumstances such as Peter's sermon on the Day of Pentecost (Acts 2:14–36); Stephen's address to the Sanhedrin (Acts 7:2–53), the longest in the book; Paul's message in the synagogue at Antioch in Pisidia (Acts 13:16–41); his farewell to the Ephesian elders at Miletus (Acts 20:18–35); his speech to the mob in Jerusalem (Acts 22:1–21); his defense before the governor Felix (Acts 24:10–21); and that before King Agrippa (Acts 26:1–29). In all, there are more than twenty-five public speeches recorded, at least in part, in the book. Almost half of these were delivered by the Apostle Paul.

A BOOK OF CITIES

Acts is a book of missions, and the gospel was taken at first to the centers of population in order that it might be dispersed from each center to the surrounding areas. Jerusalem, Samaria, and Antioch play their parts. Then the great cities of Asia Minor and of Greece come into view as the Apostle Paul travels on his extensive missionary journeys. Philippi,

Athens, Corinth, and Ephesus have important places as Paul looks toward Rome, the capital of the empire and the symbol of the outreach of the gospel to the uttermost part of the earth. The book of Acts might almost be called (as at least one writer has titled his commentary on it) from Jerusalem to Rome.

A BOOK OF RESURRECTION

The preachers and witnesses in the book of Acts were vitally aware of the fact that they served a resurrected Lord. From the beginning of the book, where we see the risen Lord himself instructing his disciples and showing "himself alive after his suffering by many infallible proofs" (Acts 1:3 NKJV), on to the very end, they preached "Jesus and the resurrection" (Acts 17:18). They had no incomplete gospel. Fully knowing and proclaiming the substitutionary death of the Lord Jesus Christ as the ground of salvation, they also proclaimed his bodily resurrection from the dead as the climax and proof of his finished redemptive work. They served a living Savior and Lord, whom they recommended to all they met. Because the messengers themselves experienced new life from their risen Lord, they had a message of life to those dead in trespasses and sins.

A BOOK OF THE HOLY SPIRIT

All through the book of Acts we observe the sovereign working of God the Holy Spirit empowering believers to be witnesses for the Lord Jesus as he had promised (Acts 1:8). This statement of the Lord just before his ascension is undoubtedly the key to the book. The promise was fulfilled at Pentecost and in all the events that followed. Power for witnessing throughout the world is the theme of the book, and that power was from the Holy Spirit, not mere human ability. Repeatedly the Holy Spirit filled the believers, directed the messengers where they should go and where they should not go, and opened men's hearts. God the Father was working; God the Son, the Lord Jesus Christ, was working, for the three Persons are all one and the selfsame God. The results were seen to be his, and the glory his. The believers were his servants, his instruments.

PREPARATION FOR WITNESSING (chapter 1)

In Acts 1 the believers are waiting for the Holy Spirit; in Acts 2 they are empowered with the Holy Spirit.

The Lord Jesus made it clear to his disciples that, following his death and resurrection, the Holy Spirit would begin new ministries in the world surpassing those he had accomplished before (compare John 7:37–39; 14:16–17; 16:7–15; Acts 1:4–8). It was therefore right and necessary for those disciples immediately after the Lord's ascension to wait for the Holy Spirit, wait for the fulfillment of the promise. There is no necessity now to wait, for the Holy Spirit has come; he is here. At Pentecost he baptized the believers into one body, the body of Christ (compare Acts 1:5 with 1 Corinthians 12:13), and filled them for Christian living and witnessing.

Returning from the Mount of Olives from which they had watched the Lord Jesus ascend to heaven, the disciples gathered for prayer and fellowship in an upper room. Many students of Scripture believe that this may have been the same upper room in which the Lord had eaten the Last Supper with his disciples.

The "one accord" (Acts 1:14) of the eleven and of the 120 believers generally led to earnest prayer and waiting upon God. During this time of waiting a successor to Judas Iscariot, the betrayer of the Lord Jesus, was chosen from the group. Although some have questioned the procedure, the believers seem to have followed the proper order as indicated in the Old Testament for discerning the leading of God (see, for example, Proverbs 16:33). After Pentecost we read no more of the casting of lots in this manner. Some have denied that Matthias was God's choice, arguing that he is never heard of again. But neither are most of the Twelve heard of again in Scripture. There is no clear indication in the record that God disapproved of what was done, but quite the contrary.

It is sometimes said that God set aside Matthias and chose Paul to be among the apostles. This is definitely a misunderstanding. Paul always asserted his special apostleship, pertaining primarily to the Gentiles. He never considered himself one of the Twelve, although he was truly an apostle, commissioned directly by the risen Lord (see Galatians 1:1–12).

THE DAY OF PENTECOST (chapter 2)

Pentecost ("fiftieth") was the Old Testament Feast of Weeks, coming on the fiftieth day after the Feast of First Fruits at the spring harvest. On that occasion the loaves made from the grain of the harvest were offered before the Lord. In the New Testament fulfillment of the Old Testament typology, the Lord Jesus Christ in his resurrection was the first fruits (1 Corinthians 15:20). Pentecost is the birthday of the church, the new body which the Lord Jesus was forming for himself (Matthew 16:18; Acts 15:14; 1 Corinthians 12:13; Ephesians 1:22–23; 2:19–3:7).

The circumstances of Pentecost clearly reveal God's sovereign planning. First, the Holy Spirit supernaturally arrived in the ordinary course of events, as the disciples came together for prayer. All the disciples had gathered together "with one accord in one place" (Acts 2:1; compare 1:14). All of a sudden "there came a sound from heaven, as of a rushing mighty wind, and . . . there appeared to them divided tongues, as of fire, and one sat upon each of them. And they were all filled with the Holy Spirit" (2:2–4 NKJV).

Second, the Holy Spirit supernaturally came when he could have the greatest impact. Because of Pentecost, many devout Jews had come to Jerusalem from "every nation under heaven" (2:5). When the Holy Spirit came upon the disciples, he enabled them to speak in languages they had not learned, so that these visitors from the different areas might hear the gospel in their own tongues.

Word spread quickly about what was happening, and soon a crowd gathered around the disciples. As people stood in wonder and began to ask questions, Peter arose and addressed them. He first announced that the day's events were a fulfillment of prophecy (compare Joel 2:28–32 with Acts 2:16–21). Peter then reminded the crowd of two facts. The first fact was the ministry of Jesus of Nazareth, who was approved of God, delivered by his purpose, slain by wicked hands, and raised from the dead. The second fact was David's foretelling of the resurrection of the Messiah, or Christ (Psalm 16:8–11).

"This Jesus," Peter continued, has "God raised up [and] exalted" (Acts 2:32–33). Further, this Jesus had sent the promised Holy Spirit as manifested that day. Therefore, he is both Lord and Christ.

Convicted by Peter's message, the crowd cried out, "What shall we do?" Peter responded, "Repent, and . . . be baptized in the name of Jesus Christ for the remission of sins; and you shall receive the gift of the Holy Spirit" (2:37–38 NKJV). Notice three key elements in Peter's reply:

1. "Repent." Repent means to turn away from sin and to submit to the Lordship of Jesus Christ. The Bible defines sin

as anything that violates God's moral character, such as pride, lying, and bitterness (see Romans 1:18–32; 1 Corinthians 6:9–10; and Galatians 5:19–21). The ultimate sin occurred in Peter's day when people rejected and killed Jesus Christ, the perfect representation of God.

No one is able to meet God's moral standards on his own. Every man, no matter how wise or good, has sinned (Romans 3:10–23). Sin leads to awful consequences: dissatisfaction, despair, and finally death, or separation from God. The only way to overcome sin and its results is to admit that one is a sinner and to accept God's remedy for sin—faith in Jesus Christ (Acts 4:12; Romans 10:9–10).

2. "And be baptized . . . for the remission of sins." Baptism confirms the reality of a person's decision to turn from sin and to follow Christ. Baptism must not be misunderstood as a condition or prerequisite for the forgiveness of sins. God is faithful to forgive someone the moment he repents and turns to Christ (1 John 1:9). Baptism is a public ceremony that announces that a person has repented, received God's forgiveness, and pledged allegiance to the Lord Jesus Christ.

3. "[You will] receive the gift of the Holy Spirit." When a person turns to Christ and accepts his authority, he becomes a new creation (2 Corinthians 5:17). The Holy Spirit enters his life and takes up permanent residence there. Nothing can ever force him out. He is the guarantee of one' salvation.

As a result of Peter's sermon, three thousand persons came to the Lord Jesus Christ that day (Acts 2:41). The promise of the Lord was being fulfilled. The Holy Spirit had come upon the believers; they had been empowered; and they had become witnesses for the Lord Jesus in Jerusalem. The closing verses of chapter 2 tell of the stirring events of those days, the awe and wonder, the joy and gladness, the fellowship and praise to God, and God's daily addition to the church.

Early Preaching in Jerusalem

Acts 3

Following the Day of Pentecost the Holy Spirit continued to use the apostles and other believers in the city of Jerusalem. The promise of the Lord Jesus (Acts 1:8) continued to be fulfilled. We read of this testimony:

> And with great power gave the apostles witness of the resurrection of the Lord Jesus: and great grace was upon them all (Acts 4:33).

The books of Acts, by its very nature, is crammed with action. Stirring events crowd upon one another without letup. These chapters (3–5) which continue the story of the early preaching in Jerusalem are no exception. Note, for example, the far-reaching results of the miracles of the healing of the lame man.

A NOTABLE MIRACLE

The miracles recorded in Acts were performed by God as evidence of the truth of the witness given by the believers. God confirmed "the word with signs following" (Mark 16:20). As we read these chapters of Acts, we need to allow ourselves to be caught up in the marvelous excitement of those days. As Paul was to say much later to Agrippa, "This thing was not done in a corner" (Acts 26:26). The events were public and they became public knowledge. In the face of the evident power of God, no one could remain neutral for long. The amazement of the populace soon gave way to belief on the part of many, opposition on the part of others. The rulers particularly were troubled about the fast-moving events because they recognized that their prestige and influence were threatened. Consequently they lost no time, after the healing of the lame man at the Beautiful Gate and Peter's words to the crowd, in taking Peter and John into custody.

"Such as I give I you," said Peter to the lame man (Acts 3:6). We cannot give what we do not have. Often since then the church has lacked the power to do for men what men cannot do for themselves. Always this lack comes from failure to depend upon the risen Lord Jesus Christ, who has sent the Holy Spirit to give power.

"In the name of Jesus Christ of Nazareth rise up and walk" (Acts 3:6). Peter made it clear as he spoke to the people that he and John had no power of their own to do anything for the lame man. The power came from Christ. "And his name through faith in his name [has] made this man strong" (Acts 3:16).

That the man had been lame and that now he could walk could not be denied by anyone. The only thing the leaders could do to stop the testimony was to try to suppress it by force, since they could not successfully refute it.

PETER AND JOHN BEFORE THE COUNCIL

Just as Peter had preached Christ before the multitude, so he now proclaimed him before the Sanhedrin, the council of religious leaders, showing from Psalm 118 that this One was the stone rejected by them, the builders, but exalted by God to be the "head of the corner" (Acts 4:11). Christ, declared Peter, is the only Savior:

> Neither is there salvation in any other: for there is none other name under heaven given among men, whereby we must be saved (Acts 4:12).

The unbelieving religious leaders commanded silence. But when God says, "Speak," and man says, "Be silent," God's servants have no choice but to speak (see Acts 4:19–20; compare Acts 5:28–29).

GREAT GRACE UPON THEM ALL

As the company of believers received Peter and John after their release, they praised God—quoting from Psalm 2—and prayed for boldness to speak of Christ. God answered their prayer (Acts 4:31). The promise of the Lord Jesus continued to be fulfilled; they were recipients of power through the Holy Spirit of God. With their enduement of power by the Holy Spirit they also experienced a oneness that led to their sharing with others all that they had.

Many have spoken of this situation in the early church as an ancient form of communism. It bears no relation to Marxist communism, which is atheistic and materialistic. There was no compulsion about what the believers did. Their actions were the outflow of Christian love. They did not demand that others share with them, as communists ordinarily do; they joyfully shared with others.

21

There is no indication that any believer was obligated to turn in all his possessions to the apostles. "Great grace was upon them all" (Acts 4:33). Each man who brought his property to the apostles did so from the inner prompting of the Spirit of God. The sin of Ananias and Sapphira was not in withholding that which was theirs; it was in pretending to give all, when they had given only a part. Genuine benevolence has its counterfeits. Ananias and his wife apparently wanted to keep part of their property for their own use, while at the same time gaining a reputation among the believers for total commitment of person and possessions.

CONTRAST IN THE CHURCH

At this point we first hear of Barnabas (Acts 4:36), who figures prominently later in the record. Here at the beginning he shows by his actions that character which is evident throughout, that "he was a good man, full of the Holy Spirit and of faith" (Acts 11:24). This man, filled with the Holy Spirit, is in contrast to the hypocrites, Ananias and Sapphira, who lied to the Holy Spirit (Acts 5:3). The judgment from God that fell upon this couple brought fear to the church and no doubt deterred others from similar sinful acts. This is reminiscent of the sin of Achan in the early days of the nation of Israel (Joshua 7:1–26).

As the preaching of the gospel continued, God continued to give evidence of the truth of the message by miraculous signs (Acts 5:12–16). The result was a rapid increase in the number of believers and great excitement in Jerusalem.

PERSECUTION AGAIN

Such events could not go unnoticed by the religious leaders. The high priest and others of the Sadducean party brought about the arrest of the apostles. We can imagine the consternation of these frantic men when they were told that the ones whom they had put in prison were no longer there, although the doors were shut and the watchmen on guard. How incredulous they must have been to be told a little later that the elusive apostles were publicly preaching in the temple courts. These religious leaders could not admit that God was working in and through the apostles. They did not know, and would not have admitted it if they had known, that an angel had opened the prison door.

As sometimes happens in the history of this mad world, the ordinary crowd had more sense than the leaders. The people at least recognized that God was somehow involved in all the unusual things that had been occurring in Jerusalem. Consequently the arresting officers had to bring the apostles this time "without violence" (Acts 5:26), "for they feared the people, lest they should have been stoned."

The Lord Jesus Christ clearly commanded obedience to the state in its proper sphere when he said, "Render therefore unto Caesar the things which are Caesar's; and unto God the things that are God's" (Matthew 22:21). When Caesar comes into conflict with God, Caesar must yield:

> Then Peter and the other apostles answered and said, "We ought to obey God rather than men" (Acts 5:29).

There is sometimes such a thing as a natural bravado, even at times a native heroism in the face of danger, but this was a supernatural boldness; this was the manifestation of the power given by the Holy Spirit. "You shall receive power," the Lord Jesus had said, and "you shall be witnesses unto me." Peter and his associates realized this. "We are His witnesses to these things," they explained, "and *so* also is the Holy Spirit whom God has given to those who obey Him" (Acts 5:32 NKJV).

The response of the council was a murderous hatred that wanted to kill the apostles as they had killed the apostles' Lord. What the outcome would have been we cannot say had it not been for the counsel of moderation given by one of their own number, Gamaliel. Different reactions have been expressed by commentators about Gamaliel's advice. Whether he spoke from an awakening awareness of spiritual truth, or whether, as seems more likely, he was only voicing the worldly wisdom for which he was noted, his words had weight with the council. "Let them alone," was the substance of his message. "Let the results prove whether they are of God or not." It is doubtful that any of that number, including Gamaliel, really believed that this preaching was from God. They evidently expected the message to fade away, as the other examples whom Gamaliel cited had passed off the scene of history.

But they could not quite leave them alone. They beat the apostles and "commanded that they should not speak in the name of Jesus, and let them go" (Acts 5:40). These rulers, who seemed to have so much power and who thought they were the guardians of the truth, might well have trembled as the apostles left their presence. How could they hope to prevail against those who rejoiced "that they were counted worthy to suffer shame for his name" and who daily "[ceased] not to teach and preach Jesus Christ" (Acts 5:41–42)? The chief priests were indeed fighting against God!

When we think of the circumstances under which those early Christians lived and witnessed for Lord Jesus, we may well ask ourselves about our testimony for him.

Stephen and Philip

Acts 6–8

The growing company of believers in Jerusalem, and consequent difficulties about the care of those in need, led to the appointment of seven men to have oversight of the "daily ministration" (Acts 6:1). While these men were primarily to have responsibility for material needs, they were also daily proclaimers of the gospel. Two in particular were outstanding: Stephen, who became the first martyr for Christ; and Philip, the evangelist of Samaria.

DEACONS CHOSEN

The occasion for the selection of the seven was the feeling on the part of the Hellenists, or Greek-speaking Jews, that their widows were being neglected. The apostles, recognizing their preeminent spiritual duties of prayer and the ministry of the Word, called for the appointment of seven men to oversee the care of temporal needs. Although the word *deacons* is not used in this passage, its root form is found in the verb translated "serve" tables (Acts 6:2). From this beginning, apparently, the office of deacon developed.

Possibly all seven appointed were Greeks, for they all had Greek names. The apostles saw to it that there was no discrimination in the distribution to those in need. There is no further mention of complaint on the part of the church.

However, the spiritual and the temporal cannot be separated. Even though the deacons were to provide for physical and material needs, they were to be men "of honest report, full of the Holy Spirit and wisdom" (Acts 6:3 NKJV). We see that they did not confine themselves to material concerns but preached tirelessly and fearlessly.

STEPHEN'S ADDRESS

The stirring address of Stephen, the longest recorded in Acts, was without question an example of the fulfillment of the promise of the Lord Jesus in Matthew 10:19–20:

> "But when they deliver you up, do not worry about how or what you should speak . . . for it is not you who speak, but the Spirit of your Father that speaks in you" (NKJV).

The Holy Spirit was indeed speaking in Stephen. To these religionists who claimed to hold so strongly to the law of Moses and to their ancestral traditions, he rehearsed the history of Israel from the time the "God of glory appeared" to Abraham (Acts 7:2). He traced the instances of God's grace to them and of their ungrateful responses.

As for Moses, who had been so prominently mentioned in their attacks upon Stephen, that great man had been misunderstood and rejected by his people also:

"But they understood not. . . . This Moses whom they re-fused, saying, Who made [you] a ruler and a judge? The same did God send to be a ruler and a deliverer by the hand of the angel which appeared to him in the bush" (Acts 7:25, 35).

By referring to Moses' prophecy of the "prophet" (Acts 7:37; compare Deuteronomy 18:15–18), Stephen drew by implication a parallel between Moses and the Lord Jesus Christ. They were opposing Christ because of their supposed respect for and obedience to Moses the same way:

"To whom our fathers would not obey, but thrust him from them, and in their hearts turned back again into Egypt" (Acts 7:39).

This is gathered up in the climactic charge:

"*You* stiffnecked and uncircumcised in heart and ears! You always resist the Holy Spirit; as your fathers *did*, so *do* you. Which of the prophets did your fathers not persecute? And they killed those who foretold the coming of the Just One, of whom you now have become the betrayers and murderers, who have received the law by the direction of angels and have not kept *it*" (Acts 7:51–53).

MARTYRDOM AND PERSECUTION

The fury of these religious leaders is almost unbelievable and indescribable. Like a pack of mad dogs they "gnashed on him with their teeth" (Acts 7:54). Stephen, the faithful witness, filled with the Holy Spirit, was permitted to see his ascended Lord, ready to receive him into his presence. The council, which should have been a solemn, deliberative body, weighing evidence carefully and deciding cases righteously, proved to be instead a cruel, murdering mob.

It is in this scene, so full of pathos and yet so graced by the presence of the Lord, and so ennobled by the forgiving prayer of the martyr, that there first comes into view the man who—by God's appointment—is largely to fill the succeeding record:

> The witnesses laid down their clothes at a young man's feet, whose name was Saul (Acts 7:58).

Later, with sorrow, this man was to think back upon this time:

> "So I said, 'Lord, they know that in every synagogue I imprisoned and beat those who believe on You. And when the blood of Your martyr Stephen was shed, I also was standing by consenting to his death, and guarding the clothes of those who were killing him'" (Acts 22:19–20 NKJV).

Not yet was any sorrow evident, however, for Saul thought that he was performing service to God (compare John 16:2). He continued without compunction on his course of making "havoc of the church" (Acts 8:3).

As occurred many times later in the history of the church, the persecution, because it scattered the believers, only prospered the spread of the gospel in the end (Acts 8:4).

MINISTRY OF PHILIP AND OTHERS IN SAMARIA

Another one of the seven deacons now comes into prominence. Up to this time the gospel had been preached in Jerusalem and presumably to some extent in "all Judea." Now the next part of the Lord's program was to be carried out:

> Philip went down to the city of Samaria, and preached Christ unto them (Acts 8:5).

Philip's preaching was blessed by God and resulted in abounding joy to a multitude of people (8:6–8).

In this section of Acts, we again find the importance of baptism as an outward sign of repentance. When the Samaritans "believed Philip as he preached the things concerning the kingdom of God and the name of Jesus Christ, both men and women were baptized" (8:12 NKJV). Other passages in Acts dealing with baptism include: 2:38–41; 8:36–38; 10:47–48; 16:30–33, and 22:12–16.

The question has often been raised concerning the necessity of the laying on of the apostle's hands for the gift of the Holy Spirit. The Holy Spirit had fallen upon the believers in Jerusalem, including the apostles, without the laying on of hands. It seems that in these transition events God was using the apostles, who had been eyewitnesses of the ministry of Christ, to confirm what the Lord Jesus had said about the opening of the kingdom of heaven. These heretofore despised Samaritans were the recipients of the Holy Spirit just as the believing Jews had been; Peter and John attested the opening of the door to them.

The experience of Simon the sorcerer is somewhat difficult to interpret. It may be that he had only an outward profession, not the inner reality of faith. Those who understand Acts 8:13 to mean that Simon had been saved believe that Peter in admonishing him later was not saying that he was lost, but that he had need of repentance and restoration to fellowship with God. We cannot be sure how deep or how genuine was Simon's plea:

> "Pray you to the Lord for me, that none of these things which you have spoken may come upon me" (Acts 8:24 NKJV).

The lesson for us is clear, that spiritual gifts are not obtained by human or material means but are freely given by God.

ON THE GAZA ROAD

While a great revival was going on in Samaria ordinary men would think it foolish for Philip to leave this scene of activity and go out to a lonely road. Here was a man, however, who was sensitive to the leading of the Holy Spirit. Because he was willing to obey, his mission was successful. The witness to one man no doubt was indirectly the cause of winning many others to the Lord Jesus Christ.

Imagine the perplexity of the Ethiopian official, who was evidently a proselyte to the Jewish religion, as he read the prophecy of Isaiah 53:7–8. This passage, written by inspiration about seven hundred years before, graphically pictured the vicarious sufferings and death of the Lord Jesus Christ. To the Ethiopian's question about the subject of the prophecy, "Philip opened his mouth . . . and preached unto him Jesus" (Acts 8:35).

The Holy Spirit had a prepared listener for a prepared messenger. The response of the Ethiopian to the Word of God was saving faith in the Lord Jesus Christ. The result was great joy. As the newly born-again Ethiopian "went on his way rejoicing" (Acts 8:39), Philip was caught away by the Spirit of God for further intensive and fruitful ministry.

It may well be that some who are reading this book have never received the one about whom the Ethiopian inquired. If that is true of you, may you too turn to him who was wounded for your transgressions and bruised for your iniquities (see Isaiah 53:5).

All we like sheep have gone astray; we have turned every one to his own way; and the Lord hath laid on him the iniquity of us all (Isaiah 53:6).

4

The Conversion of Saul

Acts 9

The conversion of Saul is recorded for the first time in Acts 9 and is repeated in Acts 22 and 26 and Galatians 1. Note how the various accounts supplement each other.

The young man named Saul (later called Paul) first appears in Acts at the scene of Stephen's martyrdom (Acts 7:58). He had been in favor of stoning Stephen to death (Acts 8:1). The thrilling story of how this misguided zealot, "breathing out threatening and slaughter against the disciples of the Lord" (Acts 9:1), became the preeminent preacher of "the faith which once he destroyed" (Galatians 1:23), is evidence of the power of God and of the truth of all the claims of the Lord Jesus Christ.

THE MISSION TO DAMASCUS

The man who later became the greatest missionary of the Lord Jesus Christ was at this time on a mission of Satan. Saul of Tarsus is an outstanding example of the fact that sincerity is not enough. He was full of zeal, but he was utterly wrong. How the Lord Jesus stopped him and turned him in an abrupt about-face is our subject.

Even those Jews who lived in distant places considered themselves in religious matters to be under the jurisdiction of the Sanhedrin in Jerusalem. The extent of Saul's hatred of the gospel of Christ is seen by his determination to make the long trip to Damascus for the express purpose of perse-cuting those who were the "disciples of the Lord" (Acts 9:1).

A LIGHT FROM HEAVEN

The light that shone from heaven upon Saul was the appear-ance of the glory of the risen Lord Jesus. In his defense before Agrippa, Paul indicated that the time of day was noon and described the light as being "above the brightness of the sun" (Acts 26:13). It was no wonder that he was blinded by it. The question that he heard from heaven suddenly and dramatically revealed the enormity of the crime that he had been committing:

"Saul, Saul, why are you persecuting Me?" (Acts 9:4 NKJV).

Every believer in the Lord Jesus Christ is a spiritual member of his body, vitally related to him, the Head. Any harm done to the least member is harm done to Christ. This truth now broke upon the heart of the stricken persecutor as he heard the further words, "I am Jesus whom you are persecuting" (Acts 9:5 NKJV).

Paul emphatically states that this was an objective appearance of the Lord Jesus Christ, not a subjective vision (see 1 Corinthians 9:1; 15:5–8; Galatians 1:11–12). He based his claim to apostleship on the fact that he had seen the risen Lord just as really as the eleven had seen him after his resurrection, and had been directly commissioned by him.

The first record tells us that the men accompanying Saul heard a voice (Acts 9:7). In his recital of this experience many years later to the mob in Jerusalem, Paul said:

"They that were with me saw indeed the light . . . but they heard not the voice of him that [spoke] at me" (Acts 22:9).

The forms of expression in the original language make the meaning clear. The terms used in the first account inform us that the men with Paul heard the sound of the voice; the other record indicates that they did not hear this sound as words. In this respect they were like those people who heard the voice of God during the earthly ministry of the Lord Jesus, and who said "that it thundered" (John 12:29).

Paul is an example of one who surrendered his life to the Lord Jesus the moment he believed in him and never turned back on his decision to follow the Lord. This is not always true of believers. Some, because of lack of understanding, incomplete teaching, or some other reason, do not yield their lives until some time after their acceptance of Christ. To such believers Paul addresses this word of exhortation:

"I beseech you therefore, brethren, by the mercies of God, that you present your bodies a living sacrifice, holy, acceptable unto God, *which is* your reasonable service" (Romans 12:1 NKJV).

He himself, the moment that he recognized the Lord Jesus, not only believed on him, but turned over his life to him, saying, "What shall I do, Lord?" (Acts 22:10).

THE VISIT OF ANANIAS

Here is another Ananias, quite different from the one en-
countered previously. God breaks down the opposition of
his godly servant who protests his command to visit Saul. "I
have heard . . . how much harm he has done," Ananias re-
monstrates with God (Acts 9:13 NKJV). "He is a chosen
vessel unto me," replies the Lord, "to bear my name before
the Gentiles, and Kings, and the children of Israel" (Acts
9:15).

When Ananias, so instructed by the Lord, finds the man
at the house of Judas on Straight Street, he greets him
without hesitation as "Brother Saul" (Acts 9:17). God had
prepared Saul to receive the visitor, even revealing Ananias'
name to him. In his address to the crowd in Jerusalem Paul
recounts what Ananias said to him:

> "Then he said, 'The God of our fathers has chosen you that
> you should know His will, and see the Just One, and hear
> the voice of His mouth. For you will be His witness to all
> men of what you have seen and heard.'" (Acts 22:14–15
> NKJV).

In a later account Paul summed up his response to all that
the Lord had done for him in these words:

> "Whereupon, O king Agrippa, I was not disobedient unto the
> heavenly vision" (Acts 26:19).

PREACHING AND CONSEQUENT PERIL IN
DAMASCUS AND JERUSALEM

The new believer in the Lord Jesus Christ did not lose time.
"Straightway he preached Christ in the synagogues, that he
is the Son of God" (Acts 9:20). His hearers must have been

amazed. They knew of his original intent in coming to their city.

Now as might be expected, the chief persecutor became the persecuted. He confounded his listeners, as Stephen had done, "proving that this Jesus is the Christ" (Acts 9:22 NKJV). Consequently he became the object of a murderous plot; but with the help of other believers he made a thrilling escape from Damascus, being let "down by the wall in a basket" (Acts 9:25). Perhaps as he descended he may have remembered Rahab and the spies (Joshua 2:15) or David's escape with Michal's help (1 Samuel 19:12). He gave more information about this escape in 2 Corinthians 11:32–33.

The stay in Arabia, mentioned by Paul in Galatians 1:1—evidently took place during the time mentioned in Acts 9:22–23. The expression "many days" is certainly sufficient to cover it. Paul did not say that he was in Arabia for three years, but that three years elapsed between the time of his conversion and his return to Jerusalem (Galatians 1:18). During that time he preached in Damascus, went away to Arabia, returned to Damascus and preached again, and then escaped from Damascus.

When Saul returned to Jerusalem he had a new problem (Acts 9:26). He tried, naturally, to have fellowship with the believers in Christ. It is not surprising that they were afraid of him, for he had fully earned the reputation of being their greatest enemy. But Barnabas, the kindly "son of consolation," as the apostles had named him (Acts 4:36), came to his aid and vouched for him to the company of believers.

Saul was not safe in Jerusalem any more than he had been in Damascus. When it became known that he was the object of an assassination plot, the believers enabled him to get away from Jerusalem. From Caesarea on the coast he departed for Tarsus, his native city in the province of Cilicia in Asia Minor. There he evidently remained for some time.

Now that the one who had been the chief persecutor had become a believer in Christ, there ensued a period of relaxation of persecution. Great blessing resulted.

PETER'S MINISTRY IN LYDDA AND JOPPA

Before the record shifts almost exclusively to the journeys and ministry of the Apostle Paul, Luke gives a further section on the work of Peter. At the end of chapter 9 we read of Peter's visit to Lydda and Joppa, and of two miracles that God performed through him in those cities.

The miracles recorded in Scripture were performed primarily to authenticate the message that was preached. It was not Peter who had the power to heal Aeneas. "Jesus Christ heals you" (Acts 9:34). The result was marvelous: "And all that dwelt at Lydda and Saron saw him, and turned to the Lord" (Acts 9:35).

The notable miracle of the raising of Dorcas (or Tabitha) at Joppa had a similar result: "And it was known throughout all Joppa; and many believed in the Lord" (Acts 9:42).

Since the completion of the Scriptures God has not desired nor needed to continue performing the same types of miracles over and over again. The message has been authenticated. God's Word is its own best evidence. It comes to each of us and makes its appeal, and we must decide.

Have you decided for the Lord Jesus Christ? Have you received him as your Savior? The same Holy Spirit who gives power to believers to live and witness for the Lord Jesus brings conviction through the Word to the hearts of those who do not know the Lord (read John 16:9–11).

Give heed to the Spirit of God as he points you to the Word of God, and accept the Lord Jesus Christ who died for you and rose again. Then like Saul, born from above, you can ask, "What shall I do, Lord?"

5

*P*eter and the Gentiles

Acts 10–12

Up to this point the gospel of Christ had gone out only to Jews and Samaritans. Although the Old Testament foretold the salvation of Gentiles, and the Lord Jesus had commanded the disciples to be his witnesses to the ends of the earth, the truth had not yet dawned upon the Jewish believers that Jew and Gentile were to be one in Christ. Paul explains in Ephesians that this was a "mystery," something not previously revealed, but made known through the apostles (Ephesians 3:1–7).

Now God uses Peter, to whom the Lord Jesus had given "the keys of the kingdom of heaven" (Matthew 16:19), to open the door to the Gentiles also. Before Christ came, the position of the Gentiles was a hopeless one indeed (see Ephesians 2:11–12). Peter learned, through the experience that God gave him on the housetop, that "God shows no partiality. But in every nation whoever fears Him, and works righteousness, is accepted by Him" (Acts 10:34–35 NKJV).

GOD'S PREPARATION OF CORNELIUS

In the record of Peter and Cornelius we see clearly the need of all men for the gospel. Some might think that Cornelius was already a believer, but the Scripture indicates otherwise (see specifically Acts 11:14). The Spirit of God had prepared his heart, but this did not constitute salvation. Why did not the angel tell Cornelius how to be saved? Because God in his sovereign grace has committed the message of the gospel to redeemed human beings, not to angels. What a responsibility this places upon us, and what a privilege! The angel told him to send for a *man* who would give the message.

Are the heathen lost? Yes, they most certainly are. The Word of God is plain (see, for example, Romans 1:18–32). There is no salvation apart from the Lord Jesus Christ. But God in grace can send a messenger. The Holy Spirit through Paul asks a series of searching questions:

> How then shall they call on him on whom they have not believed? And how shall they believe in him of whom they have not heard? And how shall they hear without a preacher? and how shall they preach, except they be sent? (Romans 10:14–15).

Peter became the first of a long line of messengers to take the gospel of Christ to the Gentiles.

GOD'S PREPARATION OF PETER

Not only did God have to prepare Cornelius to receive the message, but he had to prepare Peter to give it. While the servants from Cornelius were on their way from Caesarea, approaching Joppa where Peter was staying, God through a vision taught Peter that in Christ the distinction between Jew and Gentile has been removed. This went counter to all Peter's previous training and experience. His reply to God's command is self-contradictory: "Not so, Lord" (Acts 10:14). If I say "No" to him, is he my *Lord*?

Three times God gave Peter the vision, and then God supplied the interpretation by the arrival of the men from Caesarea. On the next day, accompanied by six Jewish believers (Acts 11:12), Peter started with them for Caesarea and Cornelius' house.

PETER IN THE HOUSE OF CORNELIUS

Entering into the home of a Gentile for the first time in his life, Peter proved that he understood the object lesson God had given him. He preached the gospel to Cornelius and his friends in the power of the Holy Spirit. "God [has] showed me," he explained, "that I should not call any man common or unclean" (Acts 10:28). The "middle wall of partition" had been broken down by the Lord Jesus Christ through his death on the cross (Ephesians 2:14).

Cornelius had assembled a ready congregation to hear the apostle's message. He expressed their eagerness by saying:

> "Now therefore are we all here present before God, to hear all the things that are commanded you by God" (Acts 10:33 NKJV).

Peter's sermon clearly set forth Christ in his death and both in the sense that they had seen what had taken place and in the sense that they told what they had seen. This witness of the believers was a corroboration of the witness of the Old Testament Scriptures:

"To Him all the prophets witness that, through His name, whoever believes in Him will receive remission of sins" (Acts 10:43 NKJV).

The outpouring of the Holy Spirit was the proof from God that the faith and experience of Cornelius and the others with him were genuine. This caused the Jewish believers who had come with Peter to marvel, but Peter had learned his lesson well. He knew that the Gentiles had received the same salvation through faith in the Lord Jesus Christ that he and the other Jewish believers had received.

PETER'S DEFENSE AT JERUSALEM

Word of Peter's preaching to the Gentiles came to Jerusalem and caused some to attack him and question his actions. In reply, Peter rehearsed the experience God had given him on the housetop, his summons by Cornelius, and God's gift of the Holy Spirit to the Gentile believers. He linked this up with what he remembered of the promise of the Lord Jesus:

"Then remembered I the word of the Lord, how He said, 'John indeed baptized with water, but you shall be baptized with the Holy Spirit'" (Acts 11:16 NKJV).

Only the manifest power of God could convince the Jewish believers and overcome their prejudice. Finally they admitted that God was willing to save Gentiles as well as Jews.

CHRISTIANS AT ANTIOCH

The record takes us back to the time of Stephen's martyrdom and indicates how the persecution at that time had caused believers to scatter into many new places. Wherever they went they witnessed to the saving power of Christ, but confined their testimony to their fellow Jews. At Antioch in Syria, however, some began to preach to the Gentiles also. Although the King James Version reads "Grecians," that is, Hellenists or Greek-speaking Jews, some manuscripts read "Greeks," that is, Gentiles. The latter reading is probably the correct one (Acts 11:20).

Hearing of these developments, the church in Jerusalem sent Barnabas to Antioch. God so mightily used this kind man that he needed to summon help. Consequently he traveled to Tarsus to get Saul, who apparently for some time had been living quietly in his native city, preparing for whatever ministry God had for him. These two friends then carried on a joint Bible-teaching ministry in Antioch for a year. It was in this city that the name *Christian* was first given to believers—little Christs, or "followers of Christ." Some interpreters believe the name may have been given at first in derision, but it became an honorable name.

PERSECUTION AGAIN IN JERUSALEM

The prophecy given through Agabus of the coming of famine caused the believers in Antioch to send relief to the believers in Judea. Barnabas and Saul were the agents to carry out this benevolent project of the Antioch church (Acts 11:27–30).

About this time persecution arose again. The Herod mentioned in this passage (Acts 12:1) was Herod Agrippa I, a grandson of Herod the Great, who had been reigning when the Lord Jesus was born, and a nephew of Herod Antipas, who reigned over Galilee at the time of the crucifixion. Herod Agrippa I was the father of Herod Agrippa II, the Agrippa mentioned later in this book (Acts 25:13).

Herod's cruelty toward the church included his killing of James the son of Zebedee, the brother of John, and his imprisonment of Peter. No doubt he expected that when he brought Peter before the people after the Passover (Acts 12:4), he too would be killed.

The experience of Peter in being delivered from prison is a wonderful evidence of the power of prayer (Acts 12:5). It is also a clear, if ironic, evidence of the unbelief of the human heart. Although the church had been praying constantly for his deliverance, they were slow to believe that God had answered their prayer. The Christians assembled at the home of Mary, the mother of John Mark, were like many of us. They called Rhoda crazy when she excitedly told them that Peter was at the door (Acts 12:15). We need to lay hold of God in faith and to keep on believing. It is not that our prayer is powerful or great, but that we are asking a great and powerful God who is able.

We read that "there was no small stir among the soldiers" (Acts 12:18) the next morning. When God is working in and through and for his people there will be a stir. Our lives are often humdrum because we hinder the work of God by our disobedience and unbelief. It is the life yielded to God that knows the really thrilling adventures in the best sense of the term.

Like so many before and after him, Herod Agrippa I thought of himself more highly than he ought to think. God's judgment fell upon him, as it always does sooner or later:

> So on a set day Herod, arrayed in royal apparel, sat on his throne and gave an oration to them. And the people kept shouting, "The voice of a god and not of a man!" Then immediately an angel of the Lord struck him, because he did not give glory to God. And he was eaten by worms and died (Acts 12:21–23).

The Word of God could not be restrained in its working. It "grew and multiplied" (Acts 12:24). The chapter closes and the transition is made to the second main division of the book by the brief notation of the return of Barnabas and Saul from Jerusalem to Antioch and of their taking John Mark along with them.

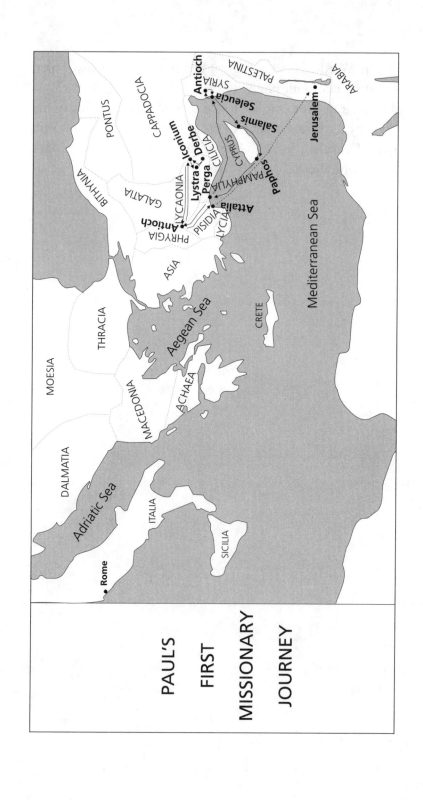

PAUL'S

FIRST

MISSIONARY

JOURNEY

6

Paul's First Missionary Journey

Acts 13–14

From Acts 13 on, Saul, or Paul as he now is known, becomes the dominant character. He tells the Corinthians later how he engaged in "journeyings often" (2 Corinthians 11:26). The magnificent Roman roads, unparalleled at the time, and which connecting all parts of the empire, and the freedom of the Mediterranean Sea from pirates, accomplished some time before by Roman naval power, were used by God, along with other means, for the spread of the gospel of Christ. Paul and his companions were untiring in their travels because they had a divine commission and were constrained by the love of the Lord Jesus Christ himself (see 2 Corinthians 5:14–21).

THE IMPORTANCE OF ANTIOCH

The book of Acts contains the record of three great missionary journeys of Paul, followed by the voyage to Rome. In
this second part of the book Antioch in Syria, rather than
Jerusalem, becomes the center of Christian activity. It was
here, as we have seen, that the name *Christian* had first been
applied to the believers. Each of Paul's missionary journeys
began at Antioch, and each ended there, except the third. On
that journey he was arrested in Jerusalem and was unable to
return and report to the home church. The first missionary
journey covered the island of Cyprus, Barnabas's home, and
a number of cities in the southern part of Asia Minor.

THE MISSIONARY CALL

Among the leaders of the church at Antioch were Barnabas
(mentioned first) and Saul (mentioned last) (Acts 13:1). God
called these two men to a special task. The beginning of the
record speaks of Barnabas and Saul, but later of Paul and
Barnabas. God in his sovereign purpose was bringing the
apostle to the Gentiles to the fore. Earlier the Lord Jesus had
said that he would send Paul to distant places among the
Gentiles (Acts 9;15; compare 22:21). Notice that God sent
these men forth, while at the same time the church sent them
(Acts 13:3–4). The verb used of the believers means, "they
let them go." In the sending forth of a true missionary God
himself must be the sender. The church's part is to recognize
the call of God and to consent to his will.

ADVENTURES IN CYPRUS

Sailing from Seleucia, the port of Antioch, Barnabas and
Saul went first to the island of Cyprus. John Mark, who was

a relative of Barnabas (Colossians 4:10), went with them as a helper.

At Paphos, on the island of Cyprus, the name Paul is first used in the record for Saul of Tarsus (Acts 13:9). Some believe that he took the name for the first time here, possibly because of the Roman proconsul, Sergius Paulus, who became a believer (Acts 13:12). It is more likely, however, that the apostle had both names from childhood, Saul being his Hebrew name (as a namesake of the first king of Israel, who was also from the tribe of Benjamin), and Paul being his Roman name, since as a native of Tarsus he was a Roman citizen from birth. Now that his ministry was to be primarily among the Gentiles in various parts of the Roman Empire, he used his Roman name exclusively. It is probable also that the name, Saul, which he had used during his Hebrew period, would have unhappy connotations for him, because under that name he had fought against God by persecuting the Christians and

Here it becomes evident that Paul was the chief speaker, as is mentioned later in the history (Acts 14:12). There is no indication that Barnabas envied Paul for assuming leadership. Some in Barnabas' position would have remonstrated that they should have the leadership by right of priority in time, and also by virtue of all that he had done to help the newer Christian. In this regard Barnabas demonstrated the Holy Spirit's assessment of him.

Barnabas was a kindly, benevolent man (Acts 11:24), who put the will of God first and accepted the place God assigned without envy or rancor. His later disagreement with Paul does not negate this.

In his rebuke of the sorcerer Bar-jesus (Elymas) and the accompanying miracle of judgment (Acts 13:9–11) Paul asserted his apostolic authority, which he had received from the risen Lord, and attested his message.

AT PISIDIAN ANTIOCH

At Perga on the southern coast of what we call Asia Minor, John Mark turned around and went back to his home in Jerusalem. We are not told his specific reason. This incident later caused dissension between Paul and Barnabas.

In Paul's day Asia Minor was a center of Greco-Roman civilization. There were many populous and wealthy cities there. We almost always associate pioneer missionaries with remote areas, but Paul brought the gospel where it had never been preached before. His strategy, under the direction of the Holy Spirit, was to touch some of the great centers of civilization from which the gospel could then radiate to outlying districts as spokes from the hub of a wheel.

It was Paul's custom as he visited various cities to preach first in the Jewish synagogue. The rulers of the synagogues ordinarily extended opportunities of speaking to visitors who seemed to be teachers. At Pisidian Antioch, being given this courtesy, Paul connected the gospel with the history of Israel. In this he seems to have been following a pattern somewhat like that of Stephen.

Paul showed the relationship of the Lord Jesus to David and to the covenant that God had made with David, and further pointed out how David by inspiration had prophesied the resurrection of the Lord Jesus Christ from the dead.

At first many were open to Paul's concluding words (Acts 13:38–39). The next week a large crowd came together to hear the preaching of the gospel, but by this time the enemy had gathered his forces. Contradiction and blasphemy met the preachers and their message. Consequently Paul and Barnabas turned to the Gentiles. What rejoicing there was among whose who were privileged to hear the good news of salvation for the first time! The Word of God was "published throughout all the region" (Acts 13:49).

WORSHIPED AND STONED

The messengers went from place to place, following the instruction of the Lord Jesus that when they were persecuted in one city they were to flee to another (Matthew 10:23). The work went on, in Iconium, in Lystra, and in Derbe. In Iconium they continued a long time (Acts 14:3), until the opposition, led by unbelieving Jews, became so strong that their lives were endangered. Many, both of Jews and Gentiles, were saved through this evangelistic campaign.

In Lystra God forwarded the work by enabling Paul to miraculously heal a crippled man. This event and its sequel show up the fickleness and instability of humanity. The miracle caused the superstitious pagans to think that Paul and Barnabas were gods who had come down to visit men, as the old Greek and Roman myths often declared. The people identified Barnabas with Zeus (KJV, "Mercurius") because he was the chief spokesman. Hermes was regarded by the Greeks as the messenger of the gods. In spite of all they could say, Paul and Barnabas could scarcely restrain these deluded polytheists from worshiping them. The missionaries exhorted their hearers to turn from these empty superstitions to the true and living God who created all things and sustains all things in his goodness (Acts 14:14–18).

Not long afterward, however, at the instigation of believing Jews from Antioch and Iconium, the people of Lystra stoned Paul, leaving him for dead (Acts 14:19). Such is earthly fame and fortune. Today a god, tomorrow an outcast; today idolized, tomorrow stoned! But if Paul and Barnabas had been seeking earthly fame and fortune they would have turned back long before this; indeed they would not have started out at all. They sought to do God's will at God's command. Because their aim was to please God, they could not be turned from their course either by men's foolish and mistaken worship or by men's equally mistaken and malicious opposition.

As they retraced their steps from Derbe through Lystra, Iconium, and Antioch, the missionaries showed the importance and value of follow-up. They confirmed "the souls of the disciples," and exhorted "them to continue in the faith" (Acts 14:22). Wherever possible the messengers of God who had first won men to Christ kept in touch with their converts, doing everything they could to assist the young Christians to grow in grace.

This is not a denial by any means of God's ability to keep those who have put their trust in him. It is God's ordained way to build up the body of Christ. We see in other parts of the New Testament how Paul nurtured those whom God had won through him by writing letters to them in which he not only gave them instruction, but also reminded them of his constant prayers on their behalf.

BACK HOME AGAIN

The missionaries who had been sent out by the church at Antioch gave a full account of their stewardship on their return. The church which had supported them was privileged to share with them in the results of the work. It was all God's doing and they gave God all the glory (Acts 14:27). Paul and Barnabas then had a long period of ministry at Antioch.

In the book of Acts we find many principles to guide us in our individual witnessing and in our corporate missionary effort. Just as the Lord Jesus Christ, risen from the dead and ascended to heaven, could continue his acts through the disciples of the first century, so he can continue his acts through you and me if we yield ourselves to him and allow his Holy Spirit to act through us.

7

The Council of Jerusalem

Acts 15

The council of Jerusalem marks a great crisis in the early Christian church, and its decision blazons forth the liberty that Paul so forcefully described in Galatians. If the Judaizers had had their way, Christianity would have become a minor Jewish sect that soon would have withered away. These false teachers could not have their way, for the Lord Jesus Christ had announced that he would build his church, and he had said, "the gates of hell shall not prevail against it" (Matthew 16:18).

A VEXING QUESTION AND ITS ANSWER

The men who came to Antioch from Judea preached an unsettling and disquieting doctrine, insisting that Gentiles had to become Jews in order to be saved. For this reason such teachers are known in history as the Judaizers. This chapter tells of the turmoil in the church from this question, and of the decision concerning the question at the Jerusalem conference.

In the beginning of the preaching of the gospel only Jews had been evangelized. Then God used Peter to open the door to the Gentiles. Nevertheless, there were still those among the Jews who insisted that Christianity was only a form of Judaism. They taught that a Gentile had to become a Jew, submitting himself to the law and to ordinances in order to be saved (Acts 15:1). One can imagine the consternation in the church at Antioch, made up mostly of Gentiles who had been rejoicing in their salvation through the Lord Jesus Christ, when these men came among them, no doubt claiming authority over the Antioch church from the church in Jerusalem.

The record speaks of the vehement "dissension and disputation" that resulted (Acts 15:2). Paul, by the grace of God, was particularly alive to the importance of the issue. Christian freedom was at stake, as he indignantly pointed out in Galatians. If the Gentile believers were to succumb to the coaxing of the Judaizers and submit to Jewish ordinances, they would be admitting that Christ was not enough, that the Savior was insufficient for salvation. Paul tells in Galatians how at Jerusalem he resisted the attempts on the part of some to compel Titus, a Gentile Christian, to submit to the ordinance of circumcision. Paul realized as few others did that surrender of such a principle would be fatal to Christian liberty (see Galatians 2:4–5). He indicates, in the passage referred to, that these Judaizers were "false brethren," not true believers at all. They should not be listened to and should be rejected by the church as spreaders of false doctrine and creators of divisions among believers. They were not furthering the cause of Christ.

THE ISSUE BEFORE THE COUNCIL

Because the apostles were in Jerusalem it seemed good to the Christians of Antioch to send a delegation there for consultation. Paul and Barnabas and certain others made the trip. Some at that time, and many in the centuries since, have intimated that there was a division between Paul and the other apostles about this question. This is completely untrue. The division that existed was not between Paul and the Twelve, but between Paul and the Twelve on the one side, and the Judaizers on the other. There was no disagreement among the apostles about the question.

Apparently in the discussion no one was denying that salvation came through the Lord Jesus Christ. The question was—does salvation come through Christ alone or through Christ plus something else? This is the great divide in Bible doctrine. This is the test of grace. Paul in Romans shows that grace, in order to be grace, must be only grace:

> And if by grace, then is it no more of works: otherwise grace is no more grace. But if it be of works, then is it no more grace: otherwise work is no more work (Romans 11:6).

Peter testified that God had put no difference between Jews and Gentiles but had saved both by his grace through faith. He asked why the believers now would want to put a grievous yoke on the Gentile Christians, a yoke, as he pointed out, "which neither our fathers nor we were able to bear" (Acts 15:10).

Peter was not talking theoretically. God through him had offered salvation to the Gentiles. Nor did Paul and Barnabas speak theoretically as they recounted what God had done through them among the Gentiles. God, declared all these men, had given the gift of the Holy Spirit to Gentiles when they believed, without any reference to the law of Moses or to ordinances. Why should these believers now take the backward step of depending upon that which could not avail?

THE DECISION OF THE COUNCIL

James seems to have been presiding at the council. This is James the Lord's brother (Galatians 1:19; Matthew 13:55), the writer of the epistle of James and the brother of Jude. He gave the summation of the evidence in what C. I. Scofield has called the most important passage dispensationally in the New Testament (Scofield Reference Edition of the Bible, page 1169).

What is God's purpose in this age? Is the church Israel, and is Israel the church? These basic questions are controverted today even among believers. What James declared is essentially what Paul also taught (Ephesians 3), that the church is a body made up of both Jews and Gentiles, distinct from both, a new entity, not clearly revealed in the Old Testament; in other words, a "mystery" (see Ephesians 3:1–6; compare also 1 Corinthians 10:32).

The quotation James used from Amos (compare Amos 9:11–12 with Acts 15:15–18) has been variously interpreted. Many take it to mean that the salvation of the Gentiles in this age is the fulfillment of the passage in Amos. Taking the full context into account, however, and James' words of introduction to the quotation, we see that he was showing a sequence of events:

(1) First, the visiting of the Gentiles to take out a people—the church.

(2) Then, the rebuilding of the tabernacle of David—the restoration of Israel.

(3) Then, the winning of the residue of men—the Millennial Age.

This is the only order that agrees with the teaching of other parts of Scripture. To make the passage in Amos refer exclusively to the present church age is to do violence to the use that James made of it (see also Romans 11:24–27).

James clearly spoke for the body of believers as opposed to the Judaizers. Paul in his Galatians says more about the private conversations of the apostles:

> For they who seemed to be somewhat in conference added nothing to me: but contrariwise, when they saw that the gospel of the uncircumcision was committed unto me, as the gospel of the circumcision was unto Peter . . . and when James, Cephas, and John, who seemed to be pillars, perceived the grace that was given unto me, they gave to me and Barnabas the right hands of fellowship; that we should go unto the heathen [i.e., the Gentiles], and they unto the circumcision (Galatians 2:6, 8–9).

The church recognized that the Gentile believers had no relationship to the law. Even the Jews, who had the law of God, could not be saved by keeping the law. Neither Jew nor Gentile could attain the favor of God by law-keeping. To attempt to force believers under the law, either as a means of justification or as a means of Christian living, was to introduce a different gospel, which was really not a gospel at all but a terrible perversion of the gospel, as Paul explains (Galatians 1:6–9).

The practices from which the Gentile believers were asked to refrain were those that would give offense. Along with these things was coupled the moral behavior which would adorn the doctrine, that believers might be pure in their lives as well as in their faith.

RESULTS OF THE LETTER

The letter from the church at Jerusalem to the believers in Antioch and the surrounding territories was a cause of great rejoicing among the Gentile believers (Acts 15:31). This was a confirmation of their liberty in Christ. They had weathered the storm of external persecution and had thrived; now they had weathered the storm of internal schism. The word that was given by letter was confirmed orally, not only by Paul and Barnabas who had been sent to Jerusalem by the Antioch church, but also by the men sent from Jerusalem—Judas, Barsabas, and Silas (Acts 15:2, 32). The last named remained in Antioch and was to have a prominent part in the later record.

BEGINNING OF THE SECOND
MISSIONARY JOURNEY

The idea for the second missionary journey originated with Paul (Acts 15:36). He and Barnabas disagreed about the latter's suggestion that they take Mark with them.

Many interpreters believe that they must take sides here; that they must pronounce judgment, declaring that Paul was right or that Barnabas was right. Human relationships are frequently so complex that we cannot state who is completely right or wrong. God uses all kinds of instruments and makes even the wrath of man, including human disagreements, to praise him. No doubt Barnabas was inclined to be more forgiving of Mark's former departure because the young man was his relative. He apparently saw potential that overrode previous shortcomings. That there was some basis for this is seen in the fact that Mark did later perform admirable service for Christ, including the writing of one of the Gospels. Years later Paul acknowledged Mark's worth (2 Timothy 4:11).

On the other hand, Paul, on the basis of previous experience, had reason to doubt Mark's usefulness. Each had valid reasons for his opinions. Who is to say who was right and who was wrong? A principle that Paul himself enunciated applies here:

> "Therefore judge nothing before the time, until the Lord come, who both will bring to light the hidden things of darkness, and will make manifest the counsels of the hearts: and then shall every man have praise of God" (1 Corinthians 4:5).

This incident is relevant to our time when we see so many different methods and procedures in the work of the Lord. Each of us must stand by our convictions as we see things in the light of God's Word, but we must be charitable toward those who have different convictions.

God is sovereign in the disposition of his workers. We look upon the disagreement of Paul and Barnabas as a tragedy, but even through this the spread of the gospel was expanded. Instead of one gospel team, there were now two. Barnabas and Mark sailed for Cyprus, while Paul and Silas traveled overland through Syria and Cilicia.

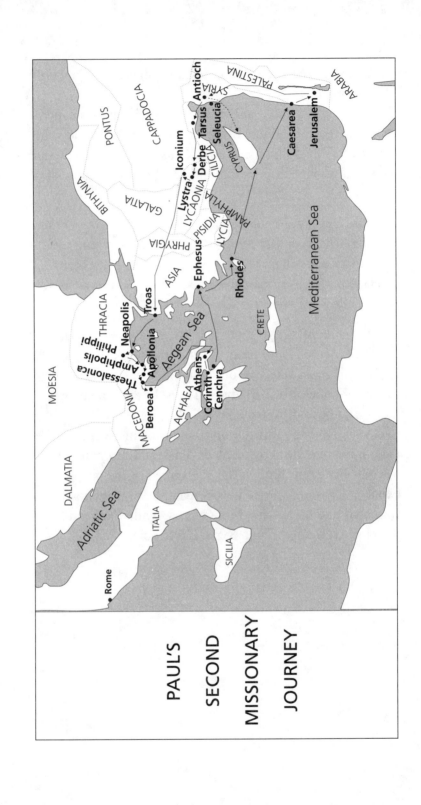

PAUL'S
SECOND
MISSIONARY
JOURNEY

8

Paul's Second Missionary Journey

Acts 15:36–18:22

On Paul's second missionary journey the gospel entered the continent of Europe. The plan appointed by the Lord Jesus continued until the message reached the ends of the earth. The risen Christ continued to act through his disciples by the power of the Holy Spirit.

THE JOURNEY, PLANNED AND UNPLANNED

Paul started the second missionary journey intending to revisit the places where he had gone on his former journey. In the purpose of God, however, this became greatly expanded and much pioneer territory was entered. The Lord led by closing doors as well as by opening them.

The second missionary journey covered at least two years, for Paul was in Corinth a year and a half (Acts 18:11) and in a number of other cities for briefer periods. It involved a much larger territory than the first journey.

At Lystra, one of the cities of the first journey, Paul and Silas were joined by the young man Timothy, who became a close friend and valuable helper throughout the remainder of the apostle's life. It is probable that Timothy's mother and grandmother (mentioned in 2 Timothy 1:5) had been saved during Paul's previous visit.

Evidently Paul wanted to enter the province of Asia to preach the gospel, but it was not yet God's time. The workers "were forbidden of the Holy Ghost to preach the word in Asia" (Acts 16:6). Paul's extended ministry in that province came some years later on his third missionary journey. In whatever way God did it, he kept them in a path toward the northwest coast of Asia Minor, permitting them to turn neither to the left hand nor to the right.

CALL TO MACEDONIA AND THE RESPONSE

At Troas, near ancient Troy, Paul received a special call in a vision of a man of Macedonia. Paul's conviction that he should minister in Macedonia was shared by all his associates. They therefore sailed from Troas, "assuredly gathering that the Lord had called us for to preach the gospel unto them" (Acts 16:10).

The emergence of the pronoun "we" at this place shows that Luke, the writer of the book, had joined Paul and his companions at Troas. We know nothing of Luke's background. He is identified in the Scripture as a physician (see Colossians 4:14) and is traditionally thought to have been a

Greek, apparently the only Gentile among the New Testament writers.

The first extensive ministry in Europe was in Philippi, a leading city in Macedonia and a Roman colony; that is, it had been settled originally by Roman veterans and their families. Since there were not enough Jews in the city to have a synagogue, worship services were held by devout women at the riverside. Here the merchant woman Lydia, originally from Thyatira in Asia Minor, heard Paul preach, and the Lord opened her heart (Acts 16:14).

TESTIMONY AND IMPRISONMENT

The preaching continued in the city. The miraculous healing of the demon-possessed slave girl brought trouble; Paul and Silas were brought before the magistrates. The charge was vague but connected to an appeal to patriotism. As Paul later pointed out, the whole trial was farcical and illegal. Nevertheless God was working out his purposes.

It is easy to sing praises to God when surroundings are pleasant and life is serene. It is not so easy in prison stocks. Yet this is what Paul and Silas did. The Holy Spirit lifted them above the circumstances. God's intervention through an earthquake brought fright to the jailer. This was no ordinary earthquake; "all the doors were opened, and every one's bands were loosed" (Acts 16:26). The jailer, who may have heard the message of Paul previously, was brought under strong conviction. "Sirs," he cried, "what must I do to be saved?" The answer was straightforward, "Believe on the Lord Jesus Christ, and you will be saved, you and your household" (Acts 16:30–31 NKJV).

Lydia and her household, the jailer and his family, and others like them formed the nucleus of the church at Philippi, which always had a close and friendly relationship with Paul and to which he addressed his epistle to the Philippians many years later during his first Roman imprisonment.

This instance is one of several occasions when Paul used his Roman citizenship to good advantage. The magistrates, realizing that they had acted illegally, feared that they would be called to account. Consequently they urged the missionaries to leave before any further trouble could arise (Acts 16:39).

THESSALONICA AND BEREA

Thessalonica, another important city of Macedonia, had a larger Jewish population than Philippi. There Paul and his associates began their ministry in the synagogue. One of the most remarkable results of Paul's stay in Thessalonica was the insight of these people into the things of God. In only one brief visit they were not only won to Christ but also instructed in the depths of Christian teaching indicated in the epistles to the Thessalonians. Dealing with some of the obscure and difficult details connected with the second coming of Christ, Paul asks, "Do you not remember that when I was still with you I told you these things" (2 Thessalonians 2:5 NKJV).

We are too inclined to limit the Holy Spirit, not realizing how much he can do in the life of a child of God. Paul was able to instruct in the deep things because he was dependent on the Holy Spirit.

So often in the apostle's travels he was opposed and persecuted by his own unbelieving race. He explains this later to the Thessalonians:

For you, brethren, became imitators of the churches of God which are in Judea in Christ Jesus. For you also suffered the same things from your own countrymen, just as they *did* from the Judeans, who both killed the Lord Jesus, and their own prophets, and have persecuted us; and they do not please God, and are contrary to all men, forbidding us to speak to the Gentiles that they might be saved, to fill up *the measure of* their sins; but wrath has come upon them to the uttermost (1 Thessalonians 2:14–16 NKJV).

Fleeing from Thessalonica, Paul and Silas came to Berea. The statement made about the people in this city has furnished a name and an incentive to innumerable Bible classes since that day:

These were more noble than those in Thessalonica, in that they received the word with all readiness of mind, and searched the scriptures daily, whether those things were so (Acts 17:11).

Opposition from Thessalonica led to Paul's having to leave this city also. Apart from his usual traveling companions, he made his way to Athens, the intellectual and cultural center of the Greek world.

DECLARATION OF THE UNKNOWN GOD

Paul, a highly educated man, must have been aware of Greek thought and literature and knew much about the past glories of Athens. But all of this was insignificant compared to its spiritual condition. He was deeply moved as he saw the prevalence of idolatry (17:16). These people who made such a fetish of philosophy—the love of wisdom—were so foolish as to bow down before things they themselves had made. The folly of worshiping human creations constituted Paul's chief indictment of idolatry (see Romans 1:22–23).

The Athenian intellectuals and dilettantes thought of Paul as a "setter forth of strange gods: because he preached unto them Jesus, and the resurrection" (Acts 17:18). Many Greek deities had names of abstract qualities, apparently the people thought "resurrection" (Greek *Anastasis*, from another form of which has come the feminine name Anastasia) was a goddess. Paul met these people where they were, building upon their religiosity and the confession of many of them that God was essentially unknown, by taking as the theme of his address on Mars' Hill the inscription on an altar in Athens: "TO THE UNKNOWN GOD" (17:23).

Some interpreters of Scripture have argued that Paul made a mistake in the type of address he gave on the Areopagus (Mars' Hill); they insist that it was too philosophical. It is out of line, however, to criticize the words of an apostle unless there is clear indication in the Scripture that he was out of God's will. This was an instance of becoming all things to all men in order to save some (see 1 Corinthians 9:22). The fact of few converts is no proof of a wrong message (Acts 17:34).

In his message Paul pointed to God as the Creator and the Judge of the world, and connected these past and future works of God by Christ's resurrection as the proof and guarantee of God's intervention in the world.

THE FIRST CORINTHIAN MINISTRY

From Athens Paul proceeded to Corinth, the capital of the Roman province of Achaia, comprising southern Greece. Corinth was a thriving commercial city. It was there that he became acquainted with Aquilla and Priscilla, who became his close friends and fellow laborers in the gospel. Many of the Jews believed in Christ, including Crispus, the ruler of the synagogue. Jesus himself encouraged Paul, assuring him that he had many people in this pagan city (Acts 18:10).

The Jews again stirred up trouble. Bringing Paul before the judgment seat of Gallio, the Roman proconsul, they accused him of teaching men contrary to the law. Gallio showed indifference to such questions, recognizing that no Roman law had been broken. This caused some of the Greeks to turn on Sosthenes, who evidently had succeeded Crispus as the leader of the Jewish synagogue. Several years later when Paul wrote his first epistle to the Corinthians, he joined the name of "Sosthenes our brother" to his own in the salutation. Could this be the same man? Possibly, for if God could save one synagogue ruler, he could surely save another. The Jews seem to have had difficulty keeping a leader of their synagogue when Paul and the gospel were around!

The second missionary journey drew to a close as Paul left Achaia, stopped briefly in Ephesus with a promise to return later, hurried to Jerusalem and greeted the church there (Acts 18:22), and then returned to his home base at Antioch.

As we read the letters addressed to some of these churches, we learn something of the earnestness of purpose of the apostle and his little company. The two epistles to the Thessalonians were written while on this journey, probably during Paul's lengthy stay in Corinth. The two letters to the Corinthians were written later, during Paul's third missionary journey. The letter to the Philippians came still later, during the apostle's first Roman imprisonment. In all of them we see his compassionate care for the churches.

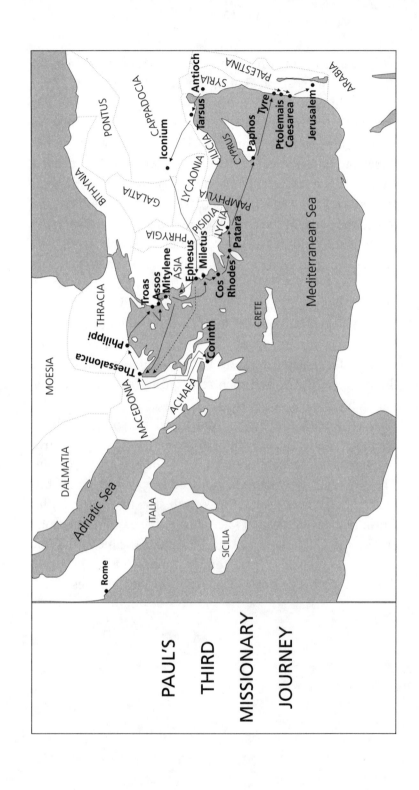

PAUL'S

THIRD

MISSIONARY

JOURNEY

9

Paul's Third Missionary Journey

Acts 18:23–21:17

Each of the great missionary journeys began at Antioch in Syria. The first and the second ended there as well. The third ended differently. On his way back to Antioch, Paul visited Jerusalem, as he had done toward the end of the previous journey; but this time he was arrested and was unable to return to Antioch.

AN EVENTFUL TERM OF MISSIONARY SERVICE

Paul's third missionary journey was even more eventful than the first two. During this journey he had a long stay in Ephesus, a leading city in the Roman province of Asia.

During this journey also (although we do not read of this in Acts) he wrote and sent his letters to the Corinthians, the Romans, and probably to the Galatians.

At the beginning of this account, Luke digresses momentarily from Paul's travels to introduce Apollos and to show how he was instructed in the things of Christ by Paul's friends Aquila and Priscilla. This is one of several instances in the book that impresses us with the fact that the work of God goes on in many places through many people. The Lord Jesus, in continuing the things that he had begun to do during his earthly ministry, was not confined to one locality. Through the Holy Spirit he was empowering a host of believers for witnessing to the uttermost part of the earth.

The narrative in this part of the book, however, centers on Paul and his ministry. We read about his stay in Ephesus and what God accomplished through him there. He brought the message of the indwelling Holy Spirit to certain disciples who knew only John's baptism. These were evidently Jews or Jewish proselytes who were confidently looking for Christ, and now that they heard the full message of the gospel, joyously accepted him.

As his practice was, Paul first spoke in the synagogue. This he did week after week for three months, until the opposition grew so strong that he had to withdraw. For two years he continued his teaching, using the school of Tyrannus. The word was spread throughout the region. "All they which dwelt in Asia heard the word of the Lord Jesus, both Jews and Greeks" (Acts 19:10). We must remember that Asia in the New Testament is not the whole vast continent, but only one province in what we now call Asia Minor.

Here is a demonstration of the power that the Lord Jesus had promised. As credentials of his ministry Paul was enabled by the Lord to perform miracles. This was God's affirmation of the message. Great excitement prevailed, many people were saved, and many renounced the Satanic devices of paganism. Paul began to make his plans to continue his travels, purposing to revisit Macedonia and Achaia, then to return to Jerusalem as he done on his previous tour, and after that, he said, "I must also see Rome" (Acts 19:21). Paul was to see Rome, but not precisely in the way or under the circumstances he anticipated at the time.

THE RIOT OF THE SILVERSMITHS

While Paul continued in Ephesus, having sent some of his party ahead into Macedonia (Acts 19:22), he was caught up in a maelstrom of opposition to the gospel. Demetrius, a Gentile, was able to inflame his fellow silversmiths because the gospel had affected all of them where they felt it, as we would say today, in their pocketbooks.

The temple of Artemis (Diana) at Ephesus was one of the reputed seven wonders of the world. The making of little silver shrines of the goddess was one of the city's leading industries. The turning of so many people "to God from idols" (compare 1 Thessalonians 1:9) threatened the livelihood of the artisans. This was the occasion of the riot described in the passage.

Paul was not permitted by his friends to confront the mob. It is interesting to see that the gospel had an impact upon some of the rulers of the province:

> And certain of the chief of Asia, which were his friends, sent unto him, desiring him that would not adventure himself into the theatre (Acts 19:31).

There is sometimes a fine distinction sometimes between bravery and folly. Paul did not lack courage, but to have gone before that howling, unreasoning mob would have been only to invite personal disaster. The people were not open to discussion of any kind; they only kept up their incessant chant, "Great is Diana of the Ephesians" (Acts 19:28, 34). Finally an official succeeded in quieting them long enough to dismiss the illegal assembly, warning them that the city was likely to be called in question by the imperial government, and pointing out that if they had any just grievances they should make use of the duly constituted law courts.

BACK TO FAMILIAR PLACES

Paul's revisiting of the churches established on his previous missionary journey is passed over very briefly. It would be interesting if we could know all the meetings and the conversations involved in the time dismissed so quickly in Acts 20:2. What reunions there must have been in Macedonia, at those churches which Paul commends so highly in his second epistle to the Corinthians (2 Corinthians 8:1–6).

In Greece (Achaia) he remained three months (Acts 20:3), possibly having his headquarters during most of that time in Corinth, the capital city of the province. As always, his bitter enemies, who considered him naturally a traitor and a renegade, sought to harm him (Acts 20:3). Instead of sailing, therefore, as he had planned, he returned overland through Macedonia, thus having opportunity to see many of the Christians there once more. The men mentioned as accompanying him (Acts 20:4) were going because of the offering collected among the Gentile believers to help the Jewish believers in Jerusalem. Paul made this an important objective in this period of his ministry, as his epistles reveal.

Luke rejoined Paul at Philippi (Acts 20:5–6), having remained there apparently for several years from the time of the original visit on the second missionary journey.

The account of the service on Troas shows us something of conditions in the early church. Eutychus, of course, was like ordinary human beings everywhere and in all ages. He cannot be blamed for his sleepiness. But the fact that Paul was able to preach so long reveals the deep hunger among the believers for the Word of God and of their great affection for the messenger God had used so greatly in their lives.

ADDRESS TO THE EPHESIAN ELDERS

The record shows us the indefatigable ministry of Paul. When we remember that he apparently suffered from kind of chronic illness (see 2 Corinthians 12:7–10), we realize more fully the sustaining grace of God for him. Determining to be in Jerusalem for the feast of Pentecost he bypassed Ephesus, but sent for the elders of that church to meet him briefly at Miletus. There on the beach he gave one of the most moving messages of his whole career.

Paul has been severely criticized by many Bible students for going to Jerusalem on this trip. He has been accused of stubbornness, self-will, and disobedience to God. While we must acknowledge that no man is sinless (except the Man Christ Jesus, who is also Lord of glory), and while we dare not say that Paul was always right in everything he did, we nevertheless ought to judge this matter in the light of the whole context. What Paul says in this address (which even many of those who criticize him accept as inspired Scripture on a par with his writings) does not sound like the deluded stubbornness of a rebellious man out of fellowship with God. He knew by revelation that "bonds and afflictions" were to come (Acts 20:23). In spite of this he had the conviction that this was a part of the course God had given him and he was determined to go forward:

"But none of these things move me, neither count I my life dear unto myself, so that I might finish my course with joy,

71

and the ministry, which I have received of the Lord Jesus, to testify the gospel of the grace of God" (Acts 20:24).

Paul's summary of his ministry in Ephesus gives us a resumé of all his work and a pattern for Christian work generally. Here was no disinterested teacher, presenting the truth and indifferently inviting his hearers to take it or leave it. No, Paul was an advocate for Christ and for his truth with his whole being. His heart was in his message. There was nothing casual about his preaching:

> "Wherefore I testify to you this day that I am innocent of the blood of all men. For I have not shunned to declare to you the whole counsel of God . . . Therefore take heed to yourselves . . . and remember, that for three years I did not cease to warn everyone night and day with tears" (Acts 20:26–31 NKJV).

ON TOWARD JERUSALEM

As Paul and his companions continued on their long journey, warnings multiplied of what lay ahead for Paul. At Tyre some of the disciples "said to Paul through the Spirit, that he should not go up to Jerusalem" (Acts 21:4). How is this statement to be interpreted? One interpretation could well be that this was a direct command of God to Paul not to go to Jerusalem. Many highly respected Bible teachers so interpret it. But this does not seem to take the whole context into account. During the period of the apostles, before the New Testament was completed, God gave some direct revelations to some of his people ("prophets"). Since Paul was a recipient of such revelations, it seems unlikely that God would tell others and not Paul what he wanted him to do. There is no indication that God revealed to Paul any direct command not to go to Jerusalem.

What God did reveal to others, as well as to Paul, was that if Paul went to Jerusalem he would be arrested and imprisoned. The other prophets who received this warning naturally, because of their love for Paul, made a plea for him not to go. Not only those in Tyre, but also Paul's friends at Caesarea, after Agabus had given his warning, entreated him not to go (Acts 21:11–12). Paul's reply on that occasion was consistent with his actions throughout the period:

> Then Paul answered, "Why are you weeping and breaking my heart? I am ready not only to be bound, but also to die in Jerusalem for the name of the Lord Jesus" (Acts 21:13 NKJV).

Although we have the right to criticize Paul, we should accept the situation as Paul's friends did:

> And when he would not be persuaded, we ceased, saying, The will of the Lord be done (Acts 21:14 NKJV).

Those who always have an answer for everything, who believe that they can always infallibly pronounce on the rightness or wrongness of the actions of other believers, would do well to criticize an apostle only where God's Word itself criticizes an apostle.

If Paul was wrong in going to Jerusalem, he is accountable to the Lord Jesus Christ. Each of us must give account of himself to God (see Romans 14:12). Let us, therefore, be sure that we are obeying the Word of God in our lives.

10

Arrested in Jerusalem

Acts 21:18–23:35

God works in strange ways. No one would have supposed that the way to Rome lay through Jerusalem. Yet in his providence the all-wise heavenly Father was preparing the scene for the climatic part of the charge of the Lord Jesus:

> "You shall be witnesses to me . . . unto the end of the earth" (Acts 1:8 NKJV).

Often we read the Bible too matter-of-factly. We need to gain or regain a sense of wonder at the wonder-working power of God and to allow ourselves to be caught up in these moving events of the spread of the gospel.

Some men would say that this was all wasted effort and wasted time; that if Paul had not gone to Jerusalem he could have gone to Rome much sooner, and not as a prisoner. Let us be careful how we judge; in fact, let us suspend judgment about this particular matter altogether and simply marvel at the delivering and all-pervasive grace of God.

PAUL IN JERUSALEM

Paul's last recorded visit to Jerusalem was filled with turmoil. After arriving in Jerusalem Paul gave a report to James and the elders of the church concerning his ministry among the Gentiles (Acts 21:18–19). Their response was to give glory to God.

The next event is another of those controversial situations that seem to cluster around Paul. Some Bible teachers are horrified that the apostles of Christian liberty would participate in any of the rituals of Judaism. It is unlikely that Paul was denying anything that he had written or spoken on the subject. He evidently was not aware of any inconsistency. This seems to have been, rather, an instance of his following the principle which he had previously laid down:

> For though I be free from all men, yet have I made myself servant unto all, that I might gain the more. And unto the Jews I became as a Jew, that I might gain the Jews; to them that are under the law, as under the law, that I might gain them that are under the law (1 Corinthians 9:19–20).

PAUL'S ARREST IN THE TEMPLE

Probably not too many people in Jerusalem would have known or recognized Paul at this time. Years had elapsed since his previous visit. However, some Jews from Asia, who would have known of his preaching in Ephesus, recognized him and stirred up the multitude against him. They made the untrue accusation that he had brought Gentiles into the temple, because they had seen Trophimus, who was from Ephesus, with him previously in the city (Acts 21:29).

Paul could be thankful for the Roman constabulary otherwise he would have been killed by the angry mob. The Roman officer in charge, without interrogating him, had him bound with chains. Later he was astonished that Paul could speak Greek, because he had jumped to the conclusion that Paul was a notorious Egyptian insurrectionist. After Paul identified himself, he was permitted to speak to the crowd.

PAUL'S DEFENSE TO THE CROWD

In his speech from the stairs in the Jerusalem street Paul rehearsed his life and his conversion, repeating what had already been placed into the record. The crowd listened as he told these things. Then he recounted a previous visit to Jerusalem, probably the first one after his conversion, and told of the words of the Lord Jesus to him on that occasion:

"Depart: for I will send you far from here to the Gentiles" (Acts 22:21 NKJV)

That was all the mob would take. When he came to that point, when he mentioned the hated Gentiles as the object of his mission, the Jews interrupted and came near to violence again. Again the Roman officer intervened and determined that he would question Paul. His plan was to use the regular method of questioning by scourging, since it was believed that this was the only way to get at the truth. Paul's question to the centurion, repeated to the chief captain, brought a change in tactics. The word Roman was like a magic word in a situation like this. The highly prized Roman citizenship that Paul possessed from birth was of great value in these circumstances. Paul did not hesitate to take advantage of it. Wishing to learn what the charges were against

Paul, the official brought him the next day before the Jewish council.

PAUL BEFORE THE SANHEDRIN

One wonders if Paul thought of Stephen on this occasion—Stephen with the shining countenance like that of an angel, Stephen endued with the boldness of the Holy Spirit. He must have. How much had happened since that long-ago-day!

It is uncertain why Paul did not recognize the high priest, who presumably would have been wearing the distinctive garb of his office. Some have surmised that Paul had poor eyesight, but we cannot be sure.

Knowing the bitter division between the Pharisees and the Sadducees, Paul appealed to a doctrine on which he and the Pharisees could agree—the fact of the resurrection of the dead. Again, some have accused Paul of compromise for identifying himself with the unbelieving Pharisees, but no compromise was involved. On this point the Pharisees were perfectly orthodox, in contrast to the rationalistic Sadducees. Paul was following the instruction of the Lord, who had defeated both the Pharisees and the Sadducees in debate (see, for example, Matthew 22:23–46) and who had told his disciples to be "wise as serpents, and harmless a doves" (Matthew 10:16).

Paul knew all along that he had broken no law, but that he could never receive a fair trial from the Jewish religious leaders, and that his only recourse, humanly speaking, was to make use of his Roman citizenship. Again Rome came to the rescue (Acts 23:10), pulling the apostle away from those who would have torn him to pieces. There is a divine irony in the thought of Caesar's legions unwittingly performing the service of God.

THE PLOT AGAINST PAUL

There is no reproach, only encouragement, in the words the
Lord Jesus spoke to Paul that night in Jerusalem:

> The following night the Lord stood by him and said, "Be of
> good cheer, Paul; for as you have testified for Me in Jerusa-
> lem, so you must also bear witness in Rome" (Acts 23:11
> NKJV).

For years Paul had been looking toward that goal. When
he wrote his epistle to the Romans while on his third missionary journey, he told of this long-held desire:

> Making request if, by some means, now at last I may find a
> way in the will of God to come to you. . . . Now I do not want
> you to be unaware, brethren, that I often planned to come to
> you (but was hindered until now), that I might have some
> fruit among you also, just as among the other Gentiles
> (Romans 1:10, 13 NKJV).

> But now having no more place in these parts, and having a
> great desire these many years to come unto you; whensoever
> I take my journey into Spain, I will come to you (Romans
> 15:23–24).

It was not to work out exactly as Paul had planned.
Nevertheless his arrival in Rome was certain; the Lord Jesus
himself had now made that clear. With this assurance Paul
could face hostile councils, murderous plots, avaricious
governors, and lackadaisical kings.

More than forty fanatical men banded together in a plot
to kill Paul, binding themselves by an oath to abstain from
food and drink until their purpose was accomplished. The
plot involved the conscious and willing connivance of the
religious leaders. Paul's nephew, in some way of which we

are not informed, learned of the plot, made it known to Paul, and then at his request revealed it to the Roman officer, Claudius Lysias.

Again we enjoy the scene of the massed power of the worldly empire protecting the lone servant of Christ. Two hundred soldiers, seventy horsemen, and two hundred spearmen were deployed to escort the prisoner to Caesarea, where he would be brought before the Roman governor.

Claudius Lysias, the chief captain, seems to have been a reasonable man. He rightly concluded, in his letter to the governor, that Paul had done nothing criminal. Paul was really in a kind of protective custody. Felix, the governor, after a preliminary questioning, remanded the prisoner for trial at such time as his accusers would appear.

Some might believe that everything was lost. Paul was a prisoner, his ministry seemingly halted, his very life in jeopardy. But Paul had a promise from the Lord, a promise that sustained him during the ensuing two years at Caesarea: "So you must also bear witness in Rome" (Acts 23:11 NKJV). Paul knew the truth of what he had written: "We walk by faith, not by sight" (2 Corinthians 5:7). How often we prefer to walk by sight, and how discouraged we become in the face of obstacles!

11

The Two Years in Caesarea

Acts 24–26

Two years seems a long time to be at the whim of a Roman governor. But God has purposes that are far above human understanding. During the whole period Paul was permitted to have the company of his friends and acquaintances. Many scholars believe it was during this time that Luke, in frequent consultation with Paul, produced his first book, the "former treatise" (see Acts 1:1), which we know as the Gospel according to Luke. At any rate we can be sure that in the economy of eternity the two years were not wasted.

PAUL BEFORE FELIX

Felix occupied the same position that Pontius Pilate had held when the Lord Jesus was crucified about thirty years earlier.

The official Roman capital of the province of Judea at that time was at Caesarea.

The chief priests lost little time in prosecuting their case against Paul. Tertullus, who spoke before the governor for them, was apparently a well-known lawyer. He began by flattering Felix and then proceeded to try to link Paul with sedition and sacrilege. He indicated that the Jewish religious leaders could have settled the case themselves if Claudius Lysias had not taken Paul out of their hands.

Paul, being permitted to speak in his own defense, gave a straightforward, unvarnished account of the events of the last twelve days. He confessed that he worshiped the God of his fathers; the difference between him and these other Jews was that he actually believed all that was written in the law and the prophets. He told of the purpose of his coming to Jerusalem, a benevolent and unselfish one (Acts 24:17).

Felix was married to Drusilla, a Jewess (Acts 24:24), who was in fact the sister of King Agrippa and Bernice. Consequently he knew something of the Jewish religion. He realized that Paul was no criminal; yet he did not set him free. We see a strange mixture in his character. He treated Paul well, permitting him as much liberty as possible for a prisoner (Acts 24:23). When Paul spoke to him of Christ, he trembled with fear, yet he would not accept the Savior. His reaction was that of so many people, putting off acceptance of Christ until another time, which unhappily never comes:

> Now as he reasoned about righteousness, self-control, and the judgment to come, Felix was afraid and answered, "Go away for now; when I have a convenient time I will call for you" (Acts 24:25 NKJV).

There never is any convenient season for accepting Christ. Soon it is too late, and there is not another opportunity to seek the Lord. Now is the accepted time.

Nevertheless Felix kept summoning Paul before him, not to be instructed in the things of Christ but as a means of extortion. Somehow the governor thought that Paul could or would pay for his release, and he was not above accepting such a bribe. Two whole years passed. Felix' term ended, and he was replaced by Porcius Festus, leaving Paul a prisoner, "to show the Jews a pleasure" (Acts 24:27).

PAUL BEFORE FESTUS

Almost as soon as Festus had been inducted into office he made a trip to Jerusalem to confer with the Jewish leaders. They renewed their old plea that Paul might be turned over to them for a religious trial, although their plan, as before, was that he should be disposed of before the trial could take place. Whatever Festus' personal character may have been, he upheld the dignity and authority of Roman law by requiring Paul's enemies to appear before him in Caesarea and to accuse Paul in open court.

As before, the Jews "laid many and grievous complaints against Paul, which they could not prove" (Acts 25:7). This is one of the most dramatic scenes in this whole dramatic book. To the formal question as to whether Paul would be willing to answer before the Jewish tribunal in Jerusalem, Paul gave a formal and decisive reply:

> So Paul said, "I stand at Caesar's judgment seat, where I ought to be judged. To the Jews I have done no wrong, as you very well know. For if I am an offender, or have committed anything deserving of death, I do not object to dying; but if there is nothing in these things of which these men accuse me, no one can deliver me to them. I appeal to Caesar" (Acts 25:10–11 NKJV).

This was the cherished, time-honored right of every Roman citizen, to appeal his case to the highest court in the empire, to the emperor himself. Festus and his council readily granted the appeal, setting the legal machinery in motion that would send Paul to Rome, there to present his case.

PAUL BEFORE AGRIPPA

The King Agrippa mentioned here was Herod Agrippa II, the son of Herod Agrippa I, whose death is described in chapter 12. During Agrippa's visit Festus told him about this troublesome prisoner who had done nothing illegal but who could not be released because of the intense feeling of the Jews against him.

Festus gives the impression throughout the account of being a man beyond his depth. He made a firm and somewhat disdainful statement of Roman justice (Acts 25:26) to the Jewish leaders, who were not particularly interested in the fine points of law; yet apparently he would have been willing to turn Paul over to them (Acts 25:20)—as a convenient way of getting rid of the problem—if Paul had not insisted on his rights as a Roman citizen. Later, as Paul spoke before Agrippa and the assembled company, Festus was only one of a long line of little men in large places in this sin-cursed world.

With all his shortcomings Festus had sense enough to realize that it would be ridiculous to send a prisoner to Caesar without having some charge against him. There were no charges against Paul, except some made-up ones, the falsity of which was perfectly obvious both to Felix and to Festus. Hence the governor did not know what to write to the imperial court. The hearing before Agrippa, therefore, took on something of the nature of a formal court hearing even though Agrippa did not have legal jurisdiction in the case.

If ever the grace of God was seen in a man it was seen in Paul. And this was one of his greatest hours. Jesus had told him that he was to bear the message before kings, and here he was, behaving with politeness and dignity, with no hint of flattery or obsequiousness. Making what seems to have been a characteristic gesture (Acts 26:1), he began his story.

The theme of this address, as well as of Paul's whole Christian life, may be summed up in his words to Agrippa: "Whereupon, O King Agrippa, I was not disobedient unto the heavenly vision" (Acts 26:19). Paul repeats the story of his conversion experience, recorded for the first time in chapter 9 and repeated in the address to the Jerusalem mob in chapter 22. Note that Paul makes everything hinge on the resurrection of Christ. This was the proof and the seal of our Lord's redemptive work on the cross. Paul showed that the Old Testament Scriptures clearly foretold the gospel:

> "I continue unto this day, witnessing both to small and great, saying none other things than those which the prophets and Moses did say should come: that Christ should suffer, and that he should be the first that should rise from the dead, and should show light unto the people, and to the Gentiles" (Acts 26:22–23).

To Festus' loud exclamation that his great learning had turned him to madness, Paul answered with dignified restraint and appealed to Agrippa's background and knowledge of events. He knew that Agrippa, who was a Jew, prided himself on his knowledge of Jewish affairs, and he pointed out that the events connected with the Lord Jesus Christ had not taken place privately but in the full glare of publicity.

This was not an academic matter with Paul, nor was it merely a personal defense. He turned it into an evangelistic appeal: "King Agrippa, do you believe the prophets? I know that you do believe" (Acts 26:27 NKJV).

The king's reply was enigmatical. Was he saying that he really was almost persuaded of the truth of the gospel, or was he cynically implying that it would take more than this to make him a Christian? Was he speaking wistfully or scornfully? Were his words serious or frivolous? We cannot be sure.

Paul, however, chose to interpret his statement seriously, for he replied with great earnestness:

"I would to God that not only you, but also all who hear me today, might become both almost and altogether such as I am, except for these chains" (Acts 26:29 NKJV).

This ended the audience, and we see as so often in human experience the tragedy of the uncommitted, even of the almost committed. Combining the responses of Felix and Agrippa, Philip P. Bliss wrote the well-known gospel song:

"Almost persuaded" now to believe;
"Almost persuaded" Christ to receive;
Seems now some soul to say,
"Go, Spirit, go Thy way,
Some more convenient day
On Thee I'll call."
"Almost persuaded," come, come today;
"Almost persuaded," turn not away;
Jesus invites you here,
Angels are lingering near,
Prayers rise from hearts so dear,
O wanderer, come.
"Almost persuaded," harvest is past!
"Almost persuaded," doom comes at last!
"Almost" cannot avail;
"Almost" is but to fail!

Sad, sad that bitter wail,
"Almost"—but lost.

Both Felix and Agrippa, as well as matter-of-fact Festus, stand in the eternal Word of God as warning examples to other men. They had the glorious opportunity to accept Christ, but they would not.

The Bible is filled with strange and unusual twists of events that portray a divine irony. All who had heard Paul were agreed that he done "nothing deserving of death or chains" (Acts 26:31 NKJV). Agrippa's conclusion might cause one to be torn between laughter and tears: "This man might have been set free if he had not appealed to Caesar" (Acts 26:32 NKJV)!

What should be the reaction of a Christian? Should one bemoan the fact that Paul had been so foolish as to appeal to Caesar? No, of course not, for that had not been a foolish action at all. It was the right thing, the only thing he could have done at the time he did.

Should we expect that Paul should be filled with remorse and bitterness? No, for Paul had the promise of the Lord Jesus that he should bear testimony in Rome, and now he could see how the Lord was going to get him there. Caesar was going to pay the bill. This was not a defeat for Paul or the gospel. "God moves in a mysterious way his wonders to perform." If we are only yielded to him, we shall become aware of his hand in all the happenings of life. Here was no blind fate against which to rail, but a heavenly Father's providence for which to give thanks.

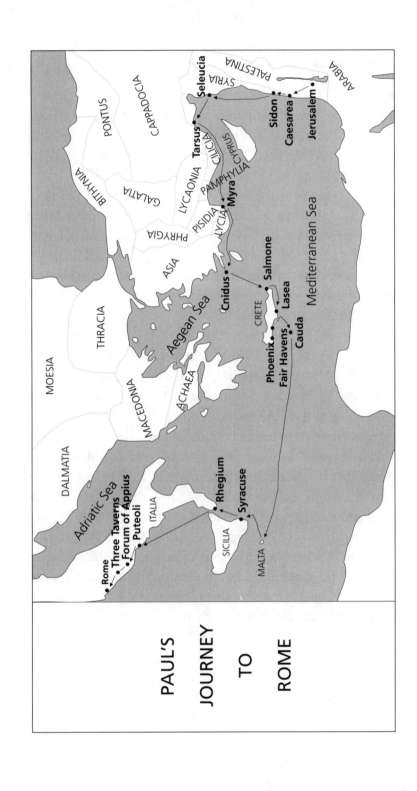

PAUL'S
JOURNEY
TO
ROME

12

The Journey to Rome

Acts 27–28

The book of Acts does not purport to tell of the ministries of all the apostles, or even to give the complete stories of those relatively few Christians whose careers it follows. We are not told of every distant place to which the gospel was taken.

Nevertheless it moves toward a climax. In chapter 13, attention shifted from Jerusalem and the evangelization of the Jews, to Antioch and the worldwide missionary effort among the Gentiles. The climax is exemplified by Rome, the imperial city. The Romans proudly boasted, "All roads lead to Rome." Conversely, all roads led from there. Once the gospel was firmly based in the capital it could spread rapidly in all directions.

In this last lesson of our study we shall note that the close of the book is in Rome, with the message still going out both to Jews and Gentiles.

BEGINNING OF THE VOYAGE

The last "we" section in the book begins with chapter 27. Paul's going to Rome had been set, and Luke accompanied him. It will help to trace the journey to Rome on the map. Paul, of course, was technically a prisoner. Julius, the centurion who was in charge of a group of prisoners on this trip, treated Paul most courteously, giving him liberties that a prisoner would not ordinarily enjoy.

This portion of the book gives a further glimpse of the extent of travel in the first century. Here we see ships plying back and forth in the Mediterranean Sea carrying both freight and passengers. Luke gives a circumstantial account of the different ships used and the different places visited.

The early part of the voyage was in the autumn, probably in the year 62. This means that Paul's arrest and his first appearance before Felix probably had been in the year 60. We know the time of year for the beginning of the voyage from the mention of the "fast" (Acts 27:9), which was the great Day of Atonement, and also from Paul's entreaty that the ship should winter at Fair Havens.

THE STORM AND SHIPWRECK

The storm that came upon them was fierce. Even the experienced sailors despaired. All hope was gone (Acts 27:20). Paul then gave encouragement, not the sort of false encouragement that the world knows as "whistling in the dark," but encouragement that was genuine because it came from God himself. An angel from God had told Paul:

"Do not be afraid, Paul. You must be brought before Caesar; and indeed God has granted you all those who sail with you" (Acts 27:24 NKJV).

In response to this, Paul's word to those with him on the ship was:

"Wherefore, sirs, be of good cheer: for I believe God, that it shall be even as it was told me" (Acts 27:25).

Believing God is the essential, no matter what the circumstances may be.

As the ship lay in shallow water with four anchors holding it, the sailors tried to save themselves by letting down the ship's boat and seeking to desert the ship and the passengers. At Paul's word to the centurion, the soldiers wanted to kill the prisoners to prevent their escaping. Julius, the centurion, who already had shown himself to be Paul's friend, kept them from their purpose, thus saving Paul's life and the lives of all the rest. As God had promised, "they escaped all safe to land" (Acts 27:44).

This was only one of the many dangers through which Paul passed in his years of service for the Lord Jesus Christ. The catalogue of his experiences that he gave to the Corinthians included, among other things, three shipwrecks and "a night and a day . . . in the deep" (2 Corinthians 11:25). That was written some years before this event.

EXPERIENCES ON MALTA

The island on which Paul and his companions were shipwrecked was the present-day Malta. The fact that the inhabitants are called barbarians simply means that they were not Greek-speaking; it does not imply that they were savages. The incident of the viper shows their superstition, as they quickly changed their opinion about Paul (Acts 28:3–6). It also is confirmation of the words of the Lord Jesus concerning the signs that would be evident in connection with the preaching of the gospel (Mark 16:18).

Another such sign was the miracle of the healing of the father of Publius, the chief man of the island. No doubt this and the ensuing miracles provided a sympathetic hearing for the gospel during the three months the travelers were on Melita.

With the coming of spring the centurion and his charges sailed on another ship, the Castor and Pollux, which had wintered on the island (Acts 28:11).

ROME AT LAST

After landing in Italy, Paul was met by Christians who were a source of great encouragement to him. At Rome he was delivered by Julius to the captain of the guard, but his status was such that he was permitted to live in a private dwelling, even though he was under constant guard. This made possible his active preaching of the gospel. His first move was to call together the leading men of the Jewish community, in order to explain his situation and to present Christ to them.

One of the unexplained circumstances is that these Jewish leaders in Rome had had no word from Judea concerning Paul. We can hardly imagine that those religious leaders who had sought his life in Judea would have failed to send a message to Rome concerning him as soon as they knew he would be sent there. It is possible that a messenger, coming at about the same time on another ship, might have been lost at sea, but this is only speculation. Whatever the cause of their not having heard about Paul, these Jewish leaders in Rome were at first willing to hear what he had to say.

It must have been a great occasion when Paul expounded the Scriptures all day to those who came:

> And when they had appointed him a day, there came many to him into his lodging; to whom he expounded and testified the kingdom of God, persuading them concerning Jesus, both out of the law of Moses, and out of the prophets, from morning till evening (Acts 28:23).

The reception was mixed, some believing and some not believing. The tragedy of Israel's unbelief as a nation is set forth in all its stark reality here at the close of Acts.

Paul had always given the Jews an opportunity to accept Christ. To the Romans he had written that the gospel "is the power of God to salvation for everyone who believes; for the Jew first, and also for the Greek" (Romans 1:16 NKJV). The statement of God's judgment upon the nation of Israel for unbelief is quoted from the book of Isaiah (Acts 28:25–27; compare Isaiah 6:9–10).

Since most of those to whom the gospel was first preached refused it, it was to be given to those who would listen:

"Be it known therefore unto you, that the salvation of God is sent unto the Gentiles, and that they will hear it" (Acts 28:28). The message of Christ was going out to the ends of the earth, as the Old Testament prophet Isaiah had prophesied and as the Lord Jesus Christ had commanded.

NOT THE END OF THE STORY

The book of Acts closes with Paul still a prisoner in Rome after two years, living "in his own hired house," receiving "all that came in unto him, preaching the kingdom of God, and teaching those things which concern the Lord Jesus Christ, with all confidence, no man forbidding him" (Acts 28:30–31).

During the two years mentioned in the passage many things occurred, even though Paul was awaiting trial. (Apparently it is not only in modern times that courts are often slow.) Among other things, he wrote his epistles to the Ephesians, to the Colossians, to Philemon, and to the Philippians. In writing to the Philippians, possibly toward the close of this two-year period, Paul told of the progress of the gospel in Rome:

> But I want you to know, brethren, that the things which happened to me have actually turned out for the furtherance of the gospel, so that it has become evident to the whole palace guard, and to all the rest, that my chains are in Christ (Philippians 1:12–13 NKJV).

At that time he looked forward confidently to his release (Philippians 1:25–26). We have reason to believe that Paul was acquitted at his trial, that he was released, and that he continued his journeys for Christ. His first epistle to Timothy and his epistle to Titus belong to that period. Still later, we believe, he was arrested again, and this time was imprisoned in a dungeon in Rome, from which he wrote his last letter, the second epistle to Timothy. None of the things mentioned in this paragraph, however, is included in the book of Acts.

Why does Acts end so abruptly? In fact, the book hardly seems to have a formal close at all. The Holy Spirit directed Luke to break off the story at this point that it might be recorded and go out while the events were still going on. This is not really the end of anything. God wants to impress upon us that there is no real close to the acts which the Lord Jesus continues to do as long as the church is in this world. The messengers are taken away one by one, but the message goes on. Throughout the centuries the risen Christ has been continuing his work through his disciples by the power of the Holy Spirit.

Bibliography

The following books are recommended to help you in your study of the book of Acts.

Gaebelein, Arno C. *The Acts of the Apostles*. Rev. ed. Neptune, N.J.: Loizeaux Brothers, 1965. *An interpretive study of the book of Acts.*

Ironside, H. A. *Acts*. Neptune, N.J.: Loizeaux Brothers, n.d. *Popular treatment. Very readable.*

Lenski, R. C. *The Interpretation of the Acts of the Apostles*. Minneapolis, Minn.: Augsburg Publishing House, 1934. *A thorough examination of the book of Acts.*

Morgan, G. Campbell. *The Acts of the Apostles*. Old Tappan, N.J.: Fleming H. Revell, 1924. *Paragraph studies by the "prince of expositors." Excellent unfolding of Acts.*

Ryrie, Charles C. *The Acts of the Apostles*. Everyman's Bible Commentary Series. Chicago: Moody Press, 1967. *Outline studies on a basic level.*

Thomas, W. H. Griffith. *Outline Studies in Acts*. Grand Rapids, Mich.: Wm. B. Eerdmans, 1956. *A scholarly work by a well-known author.*